READY-MADE
QUIZZES

In the same series

The Quiz-Setter's Quiz Book
How To Run A Quiz
Quirky Quiz Questions
The Quizmaster's Quiz Book

READY-MADE QUIZZES

Bill Murray

RIGHT WAY

CONTENTS

	PAGE
Introduction	7
Table Quizzes	9
League Quizzes	49
Quick Quizzes	129

INTRODUCTION

Welcome to *Ready-Made Quizzes*. The book contains complete quizzes in each of the three most popular formats in use in pub or club quizzes.

Table Quizzes

Section One contains ten of what I call 'Table Quizzes'. If you have ever been to a pub quiz night, the chances are that this was the type of quiz being held.

The participants firstly sort themselves into teams. Each team is given an answer sheet or pad and allocated a table number. In this type of quiz, all the teams answer the same questions.

For the sake of uniformity, the quizzes in this section all consist of four rounds of five questions per round. The number of answers required for each question corresponds to the question number: question 1 requires one answer, question 2 requires two answers and so on. This means that you will require a total of fifteen answers per round, making sixty per quiz. I have tried to vary the standard of question so that everybody will be able to answer some of them.

League Quizzes

The second type of quiz included in this book are what I refer to as 'League Quizzes'. If you have competed in a quiz league, then they will be very familiar to you.

These quizzes are played by two teams of four people. Each quiz consists of eight rounds of four questions per team. Six of the rounds are team questions where all the team members may confer before answering, and two rounds consist of individual questions to each team member in turn.

The teams toss a coin to decide whether they are Team A or Team B and the first question is directed at Team A.

Teams may only answer through their nominated captain and a time limit of thirty seconds is· usually imposed. Correct answers score two points.

Should the team be unable to answer, or give an incorrect answer, the opposing team is given a further fifteen seconds to provide a correct answer for a bonus point. During the individual rounds only a player's opposite number is allowed to answer for a bonus point. No prompting or assistance of any kind is allowed during this round.

In a quiz of this type it is always difficult to avoid an element of unfairness as the teams are answering different questions. One team invariably thinks that their opponents' questions are easier than their own. Because of this, I have tried to make the questions of a similar nature, e.g. if one team gets a pop music question to answer, then so will the other. It is also a good idea to swap over after four rounds, Team B taking the first questions in each of the last four rounds. This is to prevent one team from always having advance warning of the type of question to come.

Quick Quizzes

The third type of quiz in popular use is what I refer to as the 'Quick Quiz'. These are used where the quiz is not intended to be the main event of the evening but is used as a 'filler'. There are 31 of these included in the last section of the book, all consisting of 20 questions. Half of these are general knowledge quizzes and half are a mixture of specialist quizzes including sport, pop music and other 'novelty' subjects.

The rules and regulations above are the *usual* ones for such quizzes but they are not immutable. Equally, if you run your own quiz, you may wish to amend my questions to suit yourself: please feel free to do so. The over-riding consideration for a quiz is that it should be enjoyable for everyone taking part.

Bill Murray

TABLE QUIZ 1 – ROUND 1

Questions

1 Doctors Edwards and Steptoe pioneered which medical technique, first used successfully in the 1970s?

2 Who were the captains of these literary vessels?
(a) The Pequod. (b) The Hispaniola.

3 What would your occupation be if your work involved you with the following?
(a) MIG and TIG. (b) Mortices and tenons.
(c) Stretchers and headers.

4 Name these types of boat:
(a) Manoeuvred around the canals of Venice.
(b) Sealskin covered canoe used by Eskimos.
(c) Flat bottomed, steered with a long pole.
(d) Oval wickerwork frame covered with a leather skin.

5 Place a colour before or after each of the following words to make the name of a British butterfly. The question mark indicates where the extra word should go.
(a) Holly ? (b) ? Emperor (c) ? Tip
(d) Cabbage ? (e) Clouded ?

Answers

1 The technique for producing test tube babies.

2 (a) Captain Ahab in *Moby Dick*.
(b) Captain Smollett in *Treasure Island*.

3 (a) Welder. (b) Joiner or carpenter. (c) Bricklayer.

4 (a) Gondola. (b) Kayak. (c) Punt. (d) Coracle.

5 (a) Holly BLUE. (b) PURPLE Emperor.
(c) ORANGE Tip. (d) Cabbage WHITE.
(e) Clouded YELLOW.

TABLE QUIZ 1 – ROUND 2

Questions

1 Which well-known television character do you associate with the line 'Live long and prosper'?

2 Name two of the three British racecourses whose names begin with the letter 'F'.

3 What were the names of the real life composers played by the following actors in the following films?
(a) Richard Chamberlain in *The Music Lovers*.
(b) Kerwin Matthews in *The Waltz King*.
(c) Dirk Bogarde in *Song Without End*.

4 Which post war British prime ministers:
(a) Practised bricklaying as a hobby?
(b) Said 'A week is a long time in politics'?
(c) Resigned over the Suez crisis?
(d) Took Britain into the EEC?

5 What were the surnames of these famous 'Williams'?
(a) Cast adrift by his mutinous crew in 1789.
(b) Founded the Salvation Army.
(c) Discovered the world's sixth largest island.
(d) Died in 1984, was a famous band leader and pianist.
(e) Hanged in 1829 for grave robbing after his partner gave evidence against him.

Answers

1 Mister Spock from *Star Trek*.

2 Folkestone, Fontwell and Fakenham.

3 (a) Peter Ilyich Tchaikovsky. (b) Johann Strauss.
(c) Franz Liszt.

4 (a) Sir Winston Churchill. (b) Harold Wilson.
(c) Sir Anthony Eden. (d) Edward Heath.

5 (a) Bligh. (b) Booth. (c) Baffin. (d) Basie. (e) Burke.

TABLE QUIZ 1 – ROUND 3

Questions

1 The tree with the scientific name *Aesculus* is very popular with schoolboys. How is it more commonly known?

2 Name two of the five vegetables whose scientific name is *Brassica oleracea*.

3 Who are the only kings of England since 1066 to be:
   (a) Succeeded directly by his daughter?
   (b) Beheaded?
   (c) Killed in battle?

4 Which organisations have the following mottoes?
   (a) Be Prepared. (b) Citius, Altius, Fortius.
   (c) Blood and Fire. (d) Who Dares Wins.

5 All these questions have a 'blue' connection.
   (a) Who painted *The Blue Boy*?
   (b) Who starred in the film *Blue Hawaii*?
   (c) Which is the 'Bluegrass' state of the USA?
   (d) In which city is the Blue Mosque?
   (e) Who on radio was the voice of Bluebottle?

Answers

1 Horse chestnut (conker tree).

2 Cauliflower, cabbage, Brussels sprout, broccoli or kale.

3 (a) George VI (by Elizabeth II). (b) Charles I (in 1649).
   (c) Richard III (at Bosworth Field in 1485).

4 (a) The Scouting Association or The Girl Guides.
       [Accept either.]
   (b) The International Olympic Committee.
   (c) The Salvation Army. (d) The Special Air Service (SAS).

5 (a) Thomas Gainsborough. (b) Elvis Presley.
   (c) Kentucky. (d) Istanbul. (e) Peter Sellers.

TABLE QUIZ 1 – ROUND 4

Questions

1 Which could you have spent first in Britain:
   a 20p coin or a £1 coin?

2 Which two capital cities stand on the river Nile?

3 Name any three books by Jules Verne with a number in
   the title.

4 Complete the names of these non-league football clubs.
   (a) Witton. (b) Northwich. (c) Kidderminster.
   (d) Stafford.

5 Pop music. All these answers are place names.
   (a) Where was the House of the Rising Sun?
   (b) Where did The Monkees take the last train to?
   (c) Where did the lights all go down according to the
        Bee Gees?
   (d) Where did Daniel fly to on a plane?
   (e) Where did Tony Christie go to meet sweet Marie?

Answers

1 20p coin. 20p coins became legal tender in 1982.
   £1 coins followed in 1983.

2 Khartoum (Sudan) and Cairo (Egypt).

3 *20,000 Leagues Under the Sea, The Begum's 500 Millions,
   Around the World in 80 Days, 5 Weeks in a Balloon.*

4 (a) Witton ALBION. (b) Northwich VICTORIA.
   (c) Kidderminster HARRIERS. (d) Stafford RANGERS.

5 (a) New Orleans. In *House of the Rising Sun* by The
       Animals.
   (b) Clarkesville. In *Last Train to Clarkesville*.
   (c) Massachusetts. In *Massachusetts*.
   (d) Spain. In *Daniel* by Elton John.
   (e) Amarillo. In *Is This the Way to Amarillo?*

TABLE QUIZ 2 – ROUND 1

Questions

1 Which was the world's first antibiotic?

2 Which two letters are each worth ten points in the board game Scrabble?

3 What are the traditional nicknames given to people with the following surnames?
(a) White. (b) Miller. (c) Murphy.

4 Which four different creatures can be called an 'angora'?

5 Who were the male stars of the following films?
(a) *A Man Called Horse*.
(b) *The Man With The Golden Gun*.
(c) *The Man With Two Brains*.
(d) *The Illustrated Man*.
(e) *Man of La Mancha*.

Answers

1 Penicillin.

2 The letters Q and Z.

3 (a) Chalky. (b) Dusty. (c) Spud.

4 Goat, rabbit, cat, sheep.

5 (a) Richard Harris. (b) Roger Moore. (c) Steve Martin.
(d) Rod Steiger. (e) Peter O'Toole.

TABLE QUIZ 2 – ROUND 2

Questions

1 If you have a double X chromosome are you male or female?

2 The Arms of Great Britain are supported by a lion and a unicorn. Which two creatures support the Arms of Australia?

3 Name the three ballets written by Tchaikovsky.

4 Which are the four largest countries in the continent of Africa?

5 In which television shows were there characters with the following nicknames?
(a) Bones. (b) Potsie. (c) Digger. (d) Hawkeye.
(e) Face Man.

Answers

1 You would be female. Males have X/Y chromosomes.

2 The kangaroo and the emu.

3 *Swan Lake*, *The Sleeping Beauty* and *The Nutcracker*.

4 In order they are: Sudan, Algeria, Zaire, Libya.

5 (a) *Star Trek* (Dr Leonard McCoy).
(b) *Happy Days* (Warren Weber).
(c) *Dallas* (Willard Barnes).
(d) *MASH* (Benjamin Pearce).
(e) *The A Team* (Templeton Peck).

TABLE QUIZ 2 – ROUND 3

Questions

1 Who was the last Liberal prime minister of Great Britain?

2 Only four British banks are allowed to issue new banknotes. The Bank of England is one, name any two of the other three.

3 What have been the three most popular names of popes?

4 Which four British boxers fought Muhammed Ali in a World heavyweight title fight?

5 Which five countries apart from Britain have a coast-line on the North Sea?

Answers

1 David Lloyd George (1916–1922).

2 The Bank of Scotland, The Royal Bank of Scotland, The Clydesdale Bank.

3 John (23), Gregory (16), Benedict (15).

4 Henry Cooper, Joe Bugner, Richard Dunn, Brian London.

5 Norway, Denmark, Germany, Holland, Belgium.

TABLE QUIZ 2 – ROUND 4

Questions

1 Water, Pygmy and Common are all types of which mammal living in Britain?

2 Author Enid Blyton described her group of five as 'Famous'. Which words did she use to describe her groups of:
   (a) Seven? (b) Four?

3 Identify these three men. All have the same initials.
   (a) An American inventor, he patented the first successful sewing machine in 1851.
   (b) He was president of Rhodesia from 1964 to 1979.
   (c) The American author of the novel *Rich Man, Poor Man*.

4 What were the first two solo number one hits for:
   (a) George Michael? (b) Diana Ross?

5 What breeds are these cartoon dogs?
   (a) Scooby Doo.
   (b) Boot (from *The Perishers* strip cartoon).
   (c) Snoopy (from the *Peanuts* cartoon).
   (d) Spike (from *Tom and Jerry* cartoons).
   (e) Pluto (from Disney cartoons).

Answers

1 The shrew.

2 (a) *Secret Seven*. (b) *Adventurous Four*.

3 (a) Isaac Singer. (b) Ian Smith. (c) Irwin Shaw.

4 (a) *Careless Whisper* and *A Different Corner*.
   (b) *I'm Still Waiting* and *Chain Reaction*.

5 (a) Great Dane. (b) Old English Sheepdog. (c) Beagle.
   (d) Bulldog. (e) Bloodhound.

TABLE QUIZ 3 – ROUND 1

Questions

1 What is the major tourist attraction in the Texan town of San Antonio?

2 (a) Who introduced a 'New Look' in 1947?
   (b) Who introduced a 'New Deal' in 1933?

3 Which one word fits each pair of definitions?
   (a) To fasten to a wall, board, etc in a public place AND an upright piece of timber.
   (b) Animal skin stripped of fur AND to bombard with stones.
   (c) To strike repeatedly with heavy blows AND an enclosure for animals.

4 Which of the world's countries are divided into:
   (a) Six states? (b) Twenty-six counties?
   (c) Four provinces? (d) Twenty-three cantons?

5 What type of creatures are?
   (a) Black Widow? (b) Red Eft?
   (c) Yellow Hammer? (d) White Sussex?
   (e) Blue Point?

Answers

1 The Alamo.

2 (a) Fashion designer Christian Dior.
   (b) US President Franklin D Roosevelt.

3 (a) Post. (b) Pelt. (c) Pound.

4 (a) Australia. (b) Republic of Ireland.
   (c) South Africa. (d) Switzerland.

5 (a) Spider. (b) Newt. (c) Bird (of the Bunting family).
   (d) Hen. (e) Cat (Siamese).

TABLE QUIZ 3 – ROUND 2

Questions

1 In 1970 actor Sir Laurence Olivier became Baron Olivier. Which seaside town did he become Baron Olivier of?

2 Between which two months does British Summer Time run?

3 In which television shows were the two leading male characters called:
   (a) Napoleon Solo and Ilya Kuryakin?
   (b) Jack Regan and George Carter?
   (c) Mike Stone and Steve Keller?

4 In Greek mythology which three gods ruled the universe between them? Who was the father of all three?

5 Name the first five cities outside Europe to host the summer Olympics.

Answers

1 Brighton.

2 March until October.

3 (a) *The Man From UNCLE.* (b) *The Sweeney.*
   (c) *The Streets of San Francisco.*

4 Zeus was God of the Heavens and Earth, Poseidon was God of the Seas, Pluto (or Hades) was God of the Underworld, Cronos was the father of all three.

5 St Louis (1904), Los Angeles (1932), Melbourne (1956), Tokyo (1964), Mexico City (1968).

TABLE QUIZ 3 – ROUND 3

Questions

1 What is the name of the two-coloured oblong cake usually covered in almond paste?

2 For which two films did Glenda Jackson win an Oscar as best actress?

3 What sort of 'ologists' were the following people?
(a) Sigmund Freud. (b) Quasimodo.
(c) Heinrich Schliemann.

4 Which four different names were used by the Plantagenet kings of England?

5 By what names are the following dates known?
(a) 15th July. (b) 6th January. (c) 1st November.
(d) 24th June. (e) 11th November.

Answers

1 Battenburg.

2 *Women in Love* and *A Touch of Class*.

3 (a) Psychologist. (b) Campanologist (bellringer).
(c) Archaeologist.

4 Henry, Edward, Richard, John.

5 (a) St Swithin's Day. (b) Twelfth Night or Epiphany.
(c) All Saints' Day. (d) Midsummer Day.
(e) Armistice Day or Remembrance Day (end of World War I).

TABLE QUIZ 3 – ROUND 4

Questions

1 Which Italian composed *The William Tell Overture*?

2 What were the surnames of these famous sporting brothers?
(a) Leon and Michael from boxing.
(b) Eric and Alec from cricket.

3 Which three countries of Europe have names that begin and end with the letter 'A' (in English)?

4 Identify these famous Britons.
(a) Murdered by natives in Hawaii in 1779.
(b) Beheaded in the Tower of London in 1618.
(c) Mortally wounded in battle in 1805.
(d) Fatally injured in a motorcycle accident in 1935.

5 All these answers have an astronomical connection.
(a) What was the theme tune to the film *Breakfast at Tiffany's*?
(b) What was the title of the first number one hit for the group The Animals?
(c) What was the name of the world's first jet airliner?
(d) Which newspaper did Clark Kent work for?
(e) What was the title of the religious programme broadcast by ITV every week from 1969 until 1977?

Answers

1 Gioacchino Rossini.

2 (a) Spinks. (b) Bedser.

3 Austria, Albania, Andorra.

4 (a) Captain James Cook. (b) Sir Walter Raleigh.
(c) Admiral Horatio Nelson.
(d) T E Lawrence (Lawrence of Arabia).

5 (a) *Moon River*. (b) *House of the Rising Sun*.
(c) The De Havilland Comet. (d) *The Daily Planet*.
(e) *Stars on Sunday*.

TABLE QUIZ 4 – ROUND 1

Questions

1 What is the name of the stimulant found in tea and coffee?

2 What is the principal food of:
(a) The koala? (b) The panda?

3 Which three countries wholly in Asia have a coastline on the Mediterranean Sea?

4 In the television comedy classic *Dad's Army*, there were six regular soldiers under the command of Captain Mainwaring. Name four of them.

5 Who played the title roles in:
(a) *The Good, The Bad and The Ugly*?
(b) *The Blues Brothers*?

Answers

1 Caffeine.

2 (a) Eucalyptus leaves. (b) Bamboo shoots.

3 Syria, Lebanon and Israel. (Turkey does have a Mediterranean coastline but it is partly in Europe.)

4 The six were: Sergeant Wilson, Corporal Jones and Privates Pike, Fraser, Godfrey and Walker.

5 (a) Clint Eastwood, Lee Van Cleef, Eli Wallach.
(b) Dan Ackroyd, John Belushi.

TABLE QUIZ 4 – ROUND 2

Questions

1 Which word is used to describe a cross-breed between two animals or two plants?

2 The first and last wives of Henry VIII both had the same first name. Who were they?

3 Are these chemical elements solids, liquids or gases in their natural states?
(a) Krypton. (b) Iodine. (c) Bromine.

4 In the Bible how many of the following were there?
(a) Gospels. (b) Human beings aboard Noah's Ark.
(c) Tribes of Israel.
(d) People thrown into the fiery furnace.

5 The following artistes all had a top twenty hit with a song whose title contains the name of a day of the week. Name the song in each case.
(a) The Easybeats in 1966. (b) Blondie in 1979.
(c) Duran Duran in 1984. (d) David Bowie in 1973.
(e) The Bangles in 1986.

Answers

1 Hybrid.

2 The first was Catharine of Aragon, the last was Catharine Parr.

3 (a) Gas. (b) Solid. (c) Liquid.

4 (a) Four. (Matthew, Mark, Luke and John.)
(b) Eight. (Noah, and his wife. Their three sons and their wives.)
(c) Twelve. (Traditionally from the twelve sons of Jacob.)
(d) Three. (Shadrach, Meschach and Abednego. According to the *Book of Daniel* they survived.)

5 (a) *Friday on my Mind*. (b) *Sunday Girl*.
(c) *New Moon on Monday*. (d) *Drive in Saturday*.
(e) *Manic Monday*.

TABLE QUIZ 4 – ROUND 3

Questions

1 Which was the last of the present fifty states of the United States of America to join the Union?

2 Which famous Britons were these television shows about?
(a) *The Wilderness Years*.
(b) *The Last Place on Earth*.

3 Which three South American countries does the equator pass through?

4 Answer these 'Wizard' questions.
(a) What was the name of King Arthur's wizard?
(b) Who was known as The Welsh Wizard?
(c) Who played the Wizard of Oz in the 1939 classic film?
(d) Who formed his own pop group called Wizzard?

5 Complete the titles of these books by Agatha Christie.
(a) *Death on the ?????* (b) *Murder on the ?????*
(c) *The Mysterious Affair at ?????*
(d) *The 4:50 from ?????* (e) *Murder at the ?????*

Answers

1 Hawaii (in 1959).

2 (a) Sir Winston Churchill. (b) Captain Robert Falcon Scott.

3 Brazil, Ecuador, Colombia.

4 (a) Merlin. (b) David Lloyd George. (c) Frank Morgan.
(d) Roy Wood.

5 (a) *Death on the NILE*.
(b) *Murder on the ORIENT EXPRESS*.
(c) *The Mysterious Affair at STYLES*.
(d) *The 4:50 from PADDINGTON*.
(e) *Murder at the VICARAGE*.

TABLE QUIZ 4 – ROUND 4

Questions

1 In the stories by Joel Chandler Harris about the exploits of Brer Rabbit and Brer Fox, who is the narrator?

2 Which products are particularly associated with:
   (a) The German town of Dresden?
   (b) The Devon town of Honiton?

3 What titles did the following people take on being elevated to the Peerage?
   (a) Anthony Eden. (b) Bernard Montgomery.
   (c) Harold Macmillan.

4 What colour is:
   (a) A New York taxi? (b) A ship's starboard light?
   (c) A moonstone? (d) A motorway destination sign?

5 Which are the five football clubs in the English and Scottish leagues called 'Athletic'?

Answers

1 Uncle Remus.

2 (a) China. (b) Lace.

3 (a) Earl of Avon. (b) Viscount Montgomery of Alamein.
   (c) Earl of Stockton.

4 (a) Yellow. (b) Green. (c) White.
   (d) Blue (white lettering).

5 In England: Oldham, Wigan and Charlton.
   In Scotland: Dunfermline and Forfar.

TABLE QUIZ 5 – ROUND 1

Questions

1 In which house did Catharine Earnshaw live?

2 Which two of the nine planets did Gustav Holst NOT include in his suite entitled *The Planets?*

3 Name three films starring James Stewart whose titles contain the word 'Man'.

4 Which four different wild animals belong to the same genus (i.e. *Canis)* as the domestic dog?

5 All these answers contain the same word.
   (a) Which now annual publication first appeared in the year 1699 as an advert for pills?
   (b) What is the alternative to 'Stars and Stripes' as a nickname for the national flag of the USA?
   (c) What nickname was given to the survivors of the British expeditionary force that fought alongside the French against the Germans in World War I?
   (d) Which famous London building was known as The Coburg when it was opened in 1818?
   (e) What name is given to the thirty-nine books comprising the Jewish scriptures?

Answers

1 Wuthering Heights.

2 Pluto and Earth.

3 *The Man Who Shot Liberty Valance, Murder Man, The Man From Laramie, The Man Who Knew Too Much* and *After the Thin Man.*

4 Wolf, jackal, coyote, dingo.

5 (a) *Old Moore's Almanac.* (b) Old Glory.
   (c) The Old Contemptibles. (d) The Old Vic.
   (e) The Old Testament.

TABLE QUIZ 5 – ROUND 2

Questions

1 Which range of hills stands on the border between England and Scotland?

2 Which planets in our solar system were discovered by:
(a) J G Galle in 1846? (b) William Herschel in 1781?

3 Who were the first three batsmen to score over 8,000 runs in test cricket?

4 Who were the first four actresses to play the parts of *Charlie's Angels* in the television show of the same name?

5 All these answers contain a meteorological phenomenon (something to do with the weather!).
(a) What was the name of the best known yacht owned by former prime minister Edward Heath?
(b) What was the name of the company that employed Reginald Perrin in the television series starring Leonard Rossiter?
(c) What was the title of the famous children's book written by Kenneth Grahame?
(d) Which hit song is always associated with the North East group Lindisfarne?
(e) Jockey Brian Taylor only rode one Derby winner. It won in 1974 at odds of 50/1. What was it called?

Answers

1 The Cheviots.

2 (a) Neptune. (b) Uranus.

3 Garfield Sobers, Geoffrey Boycott and Sunil Gavaskar.

4 Farrah Fawcett-Majors, Kate Jackson, Jaclyn Smith, Cheryl Ladd. (Cheryl Ladd replaced Farrah Fawcett-Majors when she left.)

5 (a) Morning Cloud. (b) Sunshine Desserts.
(c) *Wind in the Willows*. (d) *Fog on the Tyne*.
(e) Snow Knight.

TABLE QUIZ 5 – ROUND 3

Questions

1 An alloy referred to as an 'amalgam' must always contain which metal?

2 Which two Mediterranean islands are separated by the Straits of Bonifacio?

3 Which well known people have biographies called:
(a) *Imagine*? (b) *It's hello from him*? (c) *Rich*?

4 In which sports did the following well known pairs compete?
(a) McNamara and McNamee. (b) Nash and Dixon.
(c) Rodnina and Zaitzev. (d) Ramadhin and Valentine.

5 During the 1960s, 70s and 80s there were a total of seven number one hits in the British charts whose titles began with the word 'I'm'. Can you name five of them?

Answers

1 Mercury.

2 Corsica and Sardinia.

3 (a) John Lennon. (b) Ronnie Barker. (c) Richard Burton.

4 (a) Tennis (Australian). (b) Bobsleigh (British).
(c) Ice skating (Russian). (d) Cricket (West Indian).

5 *I'm into Something Good* by Herman's Hermits.
I'm a Believer by The Monkees.
I'm Alive by the Hollies.
I'm the Leader of the Gang by Gary Glitter.
I'm Still Waiting by Diana Ross.
I'm Not in Love by 10cc.
I'm Your Man by Wham!

TABLE QUIZ 5 – ROUND 4

Questions

1 What is the pen name of author David Cornwell?

2 Which two countries lie at either end of the Khyber Pass?

3 What are the three possible states in which a volcano can exist?

4 Which countries did Britain fight against in these wars?
   (a) The Opium War. (b) The Seven Years War.
   (c) The War of Jenkin's Ear. (d) The War of 1812.

5 Identify the following people. All have the same initials.
   (a) The man who scored the goal that won the 1972 FA Cup final for Leeds United.
   (b) The writer sometimes called Lady Mallowan.
   (c) The man who regularly broadcast a radio *Letter to America*.
   (d) The Italian painter best known for his views of the waterways of the city of Venice.
   (e) The American classical composer of ballets such as *Billy the Kid, The Pied Piper* and *Appalachian Spring*.

Answers

1 John Le Carré.

2 Pakistan and Afghanistan.

3 Active, extinct or dormant.

4 (a) China (1840–1842 and also 1857–1860).
   (b) France mainly, although Austria and Russia were also in opposition (1756–1763).
   (c) Spain (1739–1741).
   (d) United States of America.

5 (a) Allan Clarke. (b) Agatha Christie. (c) Alastair Cooke.
   (d) Antonio Canaletto. (e) Aaron Copeland.

TABLE QUIZ 6 – ROUND 1

Questions

1 If somebody was described as being 'hirsute', what would they be?

2 In Roman mythology who were the God and the Goddess of Love?

3 Which acids are found in:
(a) Vinegar? (b) Lemons? (c) Bee stings?

4 What are the names of the four 'Costas' popular as holiday resorts situated on the east coast of Spain?

5 All the people being described here share the surname Brown. What are their first names?
(a) The hero of the books by Richmal Crompton.
(b) The man who accompanied John Alcock on the first ever trans-Atlantic flight.
(c) The famous landscape gardener nicknamed 'Capability'.
(d) The man executed after the raid on Harpers Ferry in 1859.
(e) A deputy leader of the Labour Party during the 1960s.

Answers

1 Hairy.

2 Cupid was the God of Love, Venus was the Goddess of Love.

3 (a) Acetic acid. (b) Citric acid. (c) Formic acid.

4 Costa Blanca, Costa Brava, Costa Del Sol and Costa Dorada.

5 (a) William Brown (from the Just William series of books).
(b) Arthur Whitten Brown. (c) Lancelot Brown.
(d) John Brown (of the song *John Brown's Body*).
(e) George Brown.

TABLE QUIZ 6 – ROUND 2

Questions

1 Who in literature was haunted by the ghost of Banquo?

2 Which two British football clubs are nicknamed The Dons?

3 Name these 'disaster' films of the 1970s.
   (a) 1970 – A home-made bomb blows a hole in the side of a passenger aircraft.
   (b) 1972 – A luxury liner is hit by a massive tidal wave.
   (c) 1974 – A group of people are trapped in a burning skyscraper.

4 Which car manufacturing companies produce models with the following names?
   (a) Samara. (b) Tipo. (c) Jetta. (d) Corolla.

5 Of the ninety-two naturally occurring chemical elements eight have a name beginning with the letter 'C'. Copper is one of them. Name another five.

Answers

1 Macbeth.

2 Wimbledon and Aberdeen.

3 (a) *Airport.* (b) *The Poseidon Adventure.*
   (c) *The Towering Inferno.*

4 (a) Lada. (b) Fiat. (c) Volkswagen. (d) Toyota.

5 Calcium, carbon, chromium, chlorine, cobalt, cadmium and caesium.

TABLE QUIZ 6 – ROUND 3

Questions

1 Which group of people became known as 'Forty-niners'?

2 (a) What is the address of the White House?
  (b) What was Sherlock Holmes' address?

3 Who were the three kings of England in the year 1066?

4 Beginning at the feet and moving up the body, place these bones in the order which you would come to them (assuming that the hands are beside the hips):
patella, clavicle, sternum, radius.

5 All these answers are one word and all begin with the same letter.
  (a) Which was the first battle of the English Civil War?
  (b) Which type of anaesthetic was first used in 1842?
  (c) What is the name of the swampy region of southern Florida?
  (d) Which Biblical character had a Hebrew name meaning 'hairy'?
  (e) What do we call a person who carries out the instructions of a will?

Answers

1 Gold prospectors in the Californian gold rush.

2 (a) 1600 Pennsylvania Avenue. (b) 221b Baker Street.

3 Edward the Confessor who was succeeded by Harold II who in turn was succeeded by William I after the Norman invasion.

4 The order is: patella (knee cap), radius (lower arm), sternum (breast bone), clavicle (collar bone).
[Award points for every bone in the correct position.]

5 (a) Edgehill. (b) Ether. (c) Everglades. (d) Esau.
  (e) Executor.

TABLE QUIZ 6 – ROUND 4

Questions

1 Where are 'some more equal than others'?

2 Who were the famous mothers of:
   (a) Liza Minelli? (b) Carrie Fisher?

3 What were the names of the dogs in:
   (a) *Peter Pan*? (b) *The Wizard of Oz*?
   (c) *Oliver Twist*?

4 These television shows were all spin offs, i.e. they are about characters who originally appeared in another show. What were the original shows in each case?
   (a) *George and Mildred.* (b) *Laverne and Shirley.*
   (c) *Bootsie and Snudge.* (d) *Terry and June.*

5 The following songs were all recorded as tributes to well known people. Who were they?
   (a) *Geno* by Dexy's Midnight Runners.
   (b) *Candle in the Wind* (original version) by Elton John.
   (c) *American Pie* by Don McLean.
   (d) *Jealous Guy* by Roxy Music.
   (e) *Happy Birthday* by Stevie Wonder.

Answers

1 *Animal Farm* in the book by George Orwell. The actual quotation from the book is 'All animals are equal but some are more equal than others'.

2 (a) Judy Garland. (b) Debbie Reynolds.

3 (a) Nana. (b) Toto. (c) Bullseye.

4 (a) *Man About The House.* (b) *Happy Days.*
   (c) *The Army Game.* (d) *Happy Ever After.*

5 (a) Geno Washington. (b) Marilyn Monroe. (c) Buddy Holly.
   (d) John Lennon. (e) Martin Luther King.

TABLE QUIZ 7 – ROUND 1

Questions

1 What can be classified according to its origins, as igneous, sedimentary or metamorphic?

2 What were the collective names given to:
   (a) Athos, Porthos and Aramis?
   (b) Caspar, Melchior and Balthasar?

3 What is the minimum number of points required to win a game in each of the following sports?
   (a) Table tennis. (b) Squash. (c) Badminton.

4 What were the character names of the well known 'servants' played on television by the following actors?
   (a) Ted Cassidy. (b) Robert Guillaume.
   (c) Lionel Stander. (d) Gordon Jackson.

5 In astrology, which creatures represent the star signs covered by the following dates?
   (a) 22nd June-22nd July.
   (b) 21st April-21st May.
   (c) 24th October-22nd November.
   (d) 23rd July-23rd August.
   (e) 22nd December-20th January.

Answers

1 Rock.

2 (a) The Three Musketeers. (b) The Three Wise Men.

3 (a) 21. (b) 9. (c) 15.

4 (a) Lurch, the butler in *The Addams Family*.
   (b) Benson, the butler in *Soap* and also in *Benson*.
   (c) Max, the chauffeur in *Hart to Hart*.
   (d) Mr Hudson, the butler in *Upstairs, Downstairs*.

5 (a) Crab (Cancer). (b) Bull (Taurus).
   (c) Scorpion (Scorpio). (d) Lion (Leo).
   (e) Goat (Capricorn).

TABLE QUIZ 7 – ROUND 2

Questions

1 Which family of American brothers were supposed to have been named after the first five Americans to go into space?

2 What would your occupation probably be if you used the following systems in your work?
   (a) The Dewey decimal system. (b) The Teeline system.

3 Do the following countries have a president, a prime minister or both?
   (a) France. (b) Brazil. (c) Canada.

4 Identify these people who *sound* as though you might find them in a greengrocer's.
   (a) The winner of the best actor Oscar in 1973 for the film *Save The Tiger*.
   (b) The comedian who plays the detective Bob Louis on television.
   (c) The victor at the 1690 Battle of the Boyne.
   (d) The first president of Zimbabwe.

5 Which artistes had hits with the following songs in the years given?
   (a) *You're Sixteen* in 1974.
   (b) *Sweet Little Sixteen* in 1958. (c) *Sixteen Tons* in 1956.
   (d) *Sixteen Reasons* in 1960. (e) *Sixteen Bars* in 1976.

Answers

1 The Tracy brothers from the puppet show *Thunderbirds*.

2 (a) Librarian (book classification). (b) Secretary (short-hand).

3 (a) Both. (b) President. (c) Prime Minister.

4 (a) Jack LEMMON. (b) Jasper CARROTT.
   (c) William of ORANGE. (d) Canaan BANANA.

5 (a) Ringo Starr. (b) Chuck Berry.
   (c) Tennessee Ernie Ford and Frankie Laine. [Accept either.]
   (d) Connie Stevens. (e) The Stylistics.

TABLE QUIZ 7 – ROUND 3

Questions

1 Of which war was Marston Moor considered to be the major battle?

2 Which two books of the Old Testament have a name beginning with the letter 'P'?

3 What exactly do the following abbreviations stand for?
(a) PS. (b) AD. (c) IE.

4 In which countries do each of these rivers reach the sea?
(a) Nile. (b) Amazon. (c) Zambezi. (d) Danube.

5 In which sports could you watch matches between teams with the following nicknames?
(a) Diamonds v Bandits. (b) Flyers v Racers.
(c) Robins v Swans. (d) Chemics v Wires.
(e) Warriors v All Stars.

Answers

1 The English Civil War.

2 *Psalms, Proverbs.*

3 (a) Post Scriptum. (b) Anno Domini. (c) Id Est.

4 (a) Egypt. (b) Brazil. (c) Mozambique. (d) Romania.

5 (a) Speedway. (b) Ice hockey. (c) Football.
(d) Rugby league. (e) Basketball.

TABLE QUIZ 7 – ROUND 4

Questions

1 What do people usually call an alligator pear?

2 What are the names of the two cartoon characters who frequently try to kill Bugs Bunny?

3 During the Hundred Years War between England and France, five different kings sat on the English throne. Name three. (Name and number required in each case.)

4 If you were served the following dishes in a restaurant, would you eat them at the beginning, in the middle, or at the end of your meal?
   (a) Mulligatawny. (b) Crêpe Suzette. (c) Gazpacho. (d) Vitello.

5 All these answers contain a single letter.
   (a) A television show starring George Peppard.
   (b) A slang name given to special agents of the FBI.
   (c) A number five hit for Paul McCartney in 1972.
   (d) A government request to a newspaper not to print certain material in the interests of national security.
   (e) The name given to armed merchant ships used to attack enemy submarines during World Wars I and II.

Answers

1 An avocado.

2 Elmer Fudd and Yosemite Sam.

3 Edward III, Richard II, Henry IV, Henry V, Henry VI.

4 (a) Beginning – soup. (b) End – pancake.
   (c) Beginning – soup. (d) Middle – veal.

5 (a) *The A Team.* (b) G Men. (c) *C Moon.* (d) D Notice.
   (e) Q Ships.

TABLE QUIZ 8 – ROUND 1

Questions

1 Which king of England reputedly lost the crown jewels in The Wash?

2 In which two countries could you spend your holidays in a region called the Tyrol?

3 Which Biblical characters gave their names to:
   (a) A person considered to be a bringer of bad luck?
   (b) A champagne bottle holding the equivalent of eight standard bottles?
   (c) The world's largest spider?

4 Identify the following people. Each has a surname which is also an occupation.
   (a) A professional darts player nicknamed The Man in Black.
   (b) The first ever winner of a Gold Disc.
   (c) Television's sixth Doctor Who.
   (d) The best known character created by author Mark Twain.

5 Who were the first five cricketers to play in one hundred test matches?

Answers

1 King John.

2 Austria and Italy.

3 (a) Jonah. (b) Methuselah. (c) Goliath.

4 (a) Alan GLAZIER. (b) Glenn MILLER.
   (c) Colin BAKER. (d) Tom SAWYER.

5 Colin Cowdrey, Clive Lloyd, Geoffrey Boycott, Sunil Gavaskar, David Gower.

TABLE QUIZ 8 – ROUND 2

Questions

1 Which was the first country to place a man-made object on the surface of the moon?

2 Which animals' names translated into English mean:
(a) River Horse? (b) Man of the Woods?

3 On television, who played the female half of:
(a) *Sapphire and Steel*? (b) *Macmillan and Wife*?
(c) *Dempsey and Makepeace*?

4 All these answers begin with the same word.
(a) What is the title of the most famous work by the author Henry Rider Haggard?
(b) Which film character appeared in films in 1933 and 1976?
(c) What name is given to the Bible authorised in 1611?
(d) In which Shakespearian play does Cordelia appear?

5 Apart from the United Kingdom, name five European countries whose national flag bears a cross (excluding Malta).

Answers

1 USSR – Lunik 2 crash landed on the moon in 1959.

2 (a) Hippopotamus. (b) Orang-utan.

3 (a) Joanna Lumley. (b) Susan St James.
(c) Glynis Barber.

4 (a) KING *Solomon's Mines*. (b) KING Kong.
(c) KING *James' Version*. (d) KING *Lear*.

5 Denmark, Finland, Greece, Iceland, Norway, Sweden and Switzerland.

TABLE QUIZ 8 – ROUND 3

Questions

1 Who was the youngest of the three Brontë sisters?

2 Which instruments are used to measure:
   (a) Strength of earthquakes?
   (b) Levels of radioactivity?

3 The World War II exploits of The Dambusters are well documented.
   (a) Who was their leader?
   (b) What was the Squadron number?
   (c) Who invented the bouncing bombs used on their missions?

4 Which are the four musical instruments that make up the brass section of an orchestra?

5 Each of these answers contains something connected with the game of poker.
   (a) In which television show did celebrities have to produce cartoons on given subjects?
   (b) In which film did Clint Eastwood play the part of an Arizona sheriff?
   (c) What was the sequel to the TV comedy show *Porridge*?
   (d) What was the name of the pet dog owned by writer Elizabeth Barrett Browning?
   (e) How were Lenny Henry, Tracy Ullman and David Copperfield collectively known on television?

Answers

1 Anne.

2 (a) Seismograph. (b) Geiger counter.

3 (a) Guy Gibson. (b) 617. (c) Barnes Wallis.

4 Trumpet, trombone, tuba, French horn.

5 (a) *Quick on the DRAW.* (b) *Coogan's BLUFF.*
   (c) *Going STRAIGHT.* (d) FLUSH. (e) *THREE OF A KIND.*

TABLE QUIZ 8 – ROUND 4

Questions

1 With the manufacture of which commodity is the name of Bessemer associated?

2 On which two horses did jockey Brian Fletcher win the English Grand National?

3 Which is the world's largest species of:
(a) Monkey? (b) Bird? (c) Rodent?

4 What is situated in each corner of a British monopoly board?

5 The following book titles all refer to a character from the book. What is the full name of the character in each case?
(a) *The Scarlet Pimpernel.* (b) *The Hobbit.*
(c) *Dr Zhivago.* (d) *Jude The Obscure.*
(e) *Lady Chatterley's Lover.*

Answers

1 Steel.

2 Red Alligator and Red Rum.

3 (a) Mandrill. (b) Ostrich. (c) Capybara.

4 Go, Jail (just visiting), Free Parking, Go To Jail.

5 (a) Sir Percy Blakeney. (b) Bilbo Baggins.
(c) Yuri Zhivago. (d) Jude Fawley.
(e) Oliver Mellors.

TABLE QUIZ 9 – ROUND 1

Questions

1 Which is the largest instrument in the string section of an orchestra?

2 The word telex is actually a shortened form of two other words. What are the two words?

3 In which country would you live if your native tongue was:
(a) Magyar? (b) Flemish? (c) Catalan?

4 Identify these people who sound as though you could find them in a menagerie:
(a) Sue Townsend's young diarist.
(b) A South African born England cricket international.
(c) The founder of the Quaker movement.
(d) The English inventor of a light bulb in the 1860s.

5 Which of the prefixes IN, IM or UN do you need to add to the following words to convert them to their opposite meanings?
(a) Polite. (b) Cautious. (c) Essential.
(d) Ethical. (e) Capable.

Answers

1 Double bass.

2 Teleprinter exchange.

3 (a) Hungary. (b) Belgium. (c) Spain.

4 (a) Adrian MOLE. (b) Allan LAMB. (c) George FOX.
(d) Joseph SWAN.

5 (a) Impolite. (b) Incautious. (c) Inessential.
(d) Unethical. (e) Incapable.

TABLE QUIZ 9 – ROUND 2

Questions

1 What term is used to describe the lowest temperature theoretically possible?

2 The supporters of King James II of England after his deposition and the members of an extremist republican group in France led by Robespierre had very similar names. What were they?

3 Which famous Americans were assassinated in:
   (a) Dallas in 1963? (b) Washington in 1865?
   (c) Memphis in 1968?

4 Which TV comedy shows featured the following couples?
   (a) Darren and Samantha Stevens.
   (b) Arthur and Beryl Crabtree.
   (c) Daphne and Norman Warrender.
   (d) Linda and Robert Cochran.

5 Which five British boxers held a World title during the 1970s?

Answers

1 Absolute zero. (0° Kelvin or −273°C.)

2 Supporters of James II were called Jacobites.
   Followers of Robespierre were called Jacobins.

3 (a) John F Kennedy. (b) Abraham Lincoln.
   (c) Martin Luther King.

4 (a) *Bewitched*. (b) *No Place Like Home*.
   (c) *Just Good Friends*. (d) *Duty Free*.

5 Ken Buchanan, John Conteh, Maurice Hope, John H Stracey and Jim Watt.

TABLE QUIZ 9 – ROUND 3

Questions

1 What is the children's division of Penguin books called?

2 Which colonels led:
   (a) The Allied prisoners of war in the film *The Bridge on the River Kwai*?
   (b) The defending forces at the Alamo?

3 In mathematics what names are given to angles that are:
   (a) Less than 90°? (b) Between 90° and 180°?
   (c) Between 180° and 360°?

4 Who played the title roles in these films?
   (a) *Bonnie and Clyde* (1967).
   (b) *Samson and Delilah* (1949).

5 Name any five countries outside the continent of Africa whose names contain the letter 'Z' (in English).

Answers

1 Puffin.

2 (a) Colonel Nicholson (played in the film by Alec Guinness.)
   (b) Colonel Will Travis.

3 (a) Acute. (b) Obtuse. (c) Reflex.

4 (a) Warren Beatty and Faye Dunaway.
   (b) Victor Mature and Hedy Lamaar.

5 Belize, Brazil, Venezuela, The Czech Republic, Switzerland and New Zealand.

TABLE QUIZ 9 – ROUND 4

Questions

1 Which letter has the shortest entry in an English dictionary?

2 What is the principal chemical element found in:
   (a) Diamonds? (b) Sand?

3 Name three books by Graham Greene with a place name in the title.

4 These athletes have all retained an Olympic title. In which events?
   (a) Peter Snell. (b) Victor Saneyev.
   (c) Bob Matthias. (d) Abebe Bikila.

5 In the titles of well known songs, how many:
   (a) Hours from Tulsa? (b) Tribes?
   (c) Days a week? (d) Miles of bad road?
   (e) Little girls sitting in the back seat?

Answers

1 The letter x.

2 (a) Carbon. (b) Silicon.

3 *Stamboul Train, England Made Me, Brighton Rock,*
   Our Man in Havana, Doctor Fischer of Geneva.

4 (a) 800 metres. (b) Triple jump. (c) Decathlon.
   (d) Marathon.

5 (a) *24 Hours from Tulsa.* (b) *2 Tribes.* (c) *8 Days a Week.*
   (d) *40 Miles of Bad Road.*
   (e) *7 Little Girls Sitting in the Back Seat.*

TABLE QUIZ 10 – ROUND 1

Questions

1 What is 270 miles long and runs from Edale to Kirk Yetholm?

2 In which two events in international gymnastics do both men and women compete?

3 In the Wild West, who was shot and killed:
(a) By Bob Ford? (b) By Sheriff Pat Garrett?
(c) While playing poker in a Deadwood Saloon?

4 From which of Shakespeare's plays are the following words taken?
(a) 'The quality of mercy is not strain'd'.
(b) 'A plague o' both your houses'.
(c) 'When shall we three meet again'.
(d) 'Age cannot wither her'.

5 The following nations all have a national flag consisting of three coloured stripes. Are they vertical stripes or horizontal stripes?
(a) France. (b) Italy. (c) Spain. (d) Belgium.
(e) Holland.

Answers

1 The Pennine Way.

2 Floor exercises and vault.

3 (a) Jesse James. (b) Billy the Kid. (c) Wild Bill Hickok.

4 (a) *The Merchant of Venice.* (b) *Romeo and Juliet.*
(c) *Macbeth.* (d) *Anthony and Cleopatra.*

5 (a) Vertical. (b) Vertical. (c) Horizontal.
(d) Vertical. (e) Horizontal.

TABLE QUIZ 10 – ROUND 2

Questions

1 For what is the name of Thomas Sheraton remembered?

2 Before the advent of the GCSE, schoolchildren in England and Wales were rewarded for their efforts with either a GCE or a CSE. What did each set of initials stand for?

3 Which wars were fought between the following years:
(a) 1899 – 1902? (b) 1936 – 1939? (c) 1853 – 1856?

4 The first *Star Trek* film was called *Star Trek – The Motion Picture*. What were the full titles of the next four?
(Star Trek 2, 3, 4 and 5 is not an acceptable answer.)

5 Identify these creatures. The initial letters of each answer spell the name of another creature.
(a) Which animal lives in a sett?
(b) Which wading bird was sacred to the ancient Egyptians?
(c) What name is commonly given to the *Hippocampus*?
(d) What is the alternative name for a snow leopard?
(e) In a song, which creature sang in Berkeley Square?

Answers

1 He was a renowned furniture maker.

2 General Certificate of Education.
Certificate of Secondary Education.

3 (a) Boer War. (b) Spanish Civil War. (c) Crimean War.

4 *Star Trek 2 – The Wrath of Khan, Star Trek 3 – The Search for Spock, Star Trek 4 – The Voyage Home, Star Trek 5 – The Final Frontier.*

5 (a) Badger. (b) Ibis. (c) Seahorse. (d) Ounce.
(e) Nightingale.
The initial letters of these answers spell BISON.

TABLE QUIZ 10 – ROUND 3

Questions

1 Which famous harbour is situated on the island of Oahu?

2 For which diseases did (a) Edward Jenner and
 (b) Jonas Salk develop an effective vaccine?

3 Which one word names are given to:
 (a) The study of God?
 (b) The study of the structure and form of the human body?
 (c) The study of the relationship between living things and the environment in which they live?

4 These people all have the same surname. What are their first names?
 (a) The founder of the Mormon religion.
 (b) He declared Rhodesia independent.
 (c) A Wimbledon singles champion in 1972.
 (d) A poet whose real first name was Florence.

5 All these answers contain a month of the year.
 (a) One of the guests at the Mad Hatter's tea party.
 (b) Name given to the World War II attempt to murder Hitler.
 (c) The uprising which led to the formation of the USSR.
 (d) The recording artiste who had a 1976 top ten hit with the song *Summer of my Life*.
 (e) One of the stars of the TV comedy show *Happy Ever After*.

Answers

1 Pearl Harbor.

2 (a) Smallpox. (b) Polio.

3 (a) Theology. (b) Anatomy. (c) Ecology.

4 All are named Smith: (a) Joseph. (b) Ian. (c) Stan.
 (d) Stevie.

5 (a) The MARCH Hare. (b) The JULY Plot.
 (c) The OCTOBER Revolution. (d) Simon MAY.
 (e) JUNE Whitfield.

TABLE QUIZ 10 – ROUND 4

Questions

1 Which part of the British Army are known as 'Sappers'?

2 What are the names of the two central characters in the Charles Dickens novel *A Tale of Two Cities*?

3 In which modern countries could you visit the ruins of these ancient civilisations?
(a) Aztec. (b) Inca. (c) Carthaginian.

4 Name a hit record for each of the following whose title contains the name of a type of nautical transport.
(a) The Beatles. (b) Lulu. (c) The Beach Boys.
(d) Erasure.

5 The following people were all sporting World champions during the 1980s. Name their sports or games.
(a) Norman Dagley. (b) Egon Muller.
(c) Terry Sullivan. (d) Brian Orser.
(e) Sergei Bubka.

Answers

1 The Royal Engineers.

2 Charles Darnay and Sidney Carton.

3 (a) Mexico. (b) Peru. (c) Tunisia.

4 (a) *Yellow Submarine.* (b) *The Boat That I Row.*
(c) *Sloop John B.* (d) *Ship of Fools.*

5 (a) Billiards. (b) Speedway. (c) Bowls. (d) Ice skating.
(e) Pole vault.

LEAGUE QUIZ 1
ROUND 1– TEAM QUESTIONS

TEAM A
Questions

1 Which letter is represented in Morse code by a single dot?

2 Which island country has two official languages, Greek and Turkish?

3 The USA launched an orbiting space station in 1973. What was it called?

4 Which sign of the zodiac covers part of both April and May?

TEAM B

1 Which letter is represented in Morse code by a single dash?

2 Which island country has two official languages, Sinhalese and Tamil?

3 The USA launched its first Space Shuttle in 1981. What was it called?

4 Which sign of the zodiac covers part of both May and June?

Answers

1 The letter 'E'.

2 Cyprus.

3 Skylab.

4 Taurus.

1 The letter 'T'.

2 Sri Lanka.

3 Columbia.

4 Gemini.

LEAGUE QUIZ 1
ROUND 2 – TEAM QUESTIONS

TEAM A
Questions

1 Which team did Sunderland play on their 1973 appearance in the FA Cup final?

2 Lester Pearson was prime minister of which country during the 1960s?

3 Who was the author of the *Foundation* series of science fiction novels?

4 In which television comedy series did Leonard Rossiter play the part of a supermarket manager?

TEAM B

1 Which team did Newcastle play on their 1974 appearance in the FA Cup final?

2 Keith Holyoake was prime minister of which country during the 1960s?

3 Who was the author of the *Dune* series of science fiction novels?

4 In which television comedy series did Bruce Forsyth play the part of a supermarket manager?

Answers

1 Leeds United.

2 Canada.

3 Isaac Azimov.

4 *Tripper's Day.*

1 Liverpool.

2 New Zealand.

3 Frank Herbert.

4 *Slinger's Day.*

LEAGUE QUIZ 1
ROUND 3 – INDIVIDUAL QUESTIONS

TEAM A
Questions

1 Which letter of the Greek alphabet equates to the English letter 'K'?

2 'Yenisey' and 'Irtysh' are both major examples of which kind of geographical feature?

3 Name the well known daily newspaper strip cartoon drawn by Maurice Dodd.

4 In which year was Prince Charles born?

TEAM B

1 Which letter of the Greek alphabet equates to the English letter 'S'?

2 'Thar' and 'Mojave' are major examples of which kind of geographical feature?

3 Name the well known daily newspaper strip cartoon drawn by Roger Kettle and Andrew Christine.

4 In which year was Prince Edward born?

Answers

1 Kappa.

2 Rivers.

3 *The Perishers.*

4 1948.

1 Sigma.

2 Deserts.

3 *Beau Peep*.

4 1964.

LEAGUE QUIZ 1
ROUND 4 – TEAM QUESTIONS

TEAM A
Questions

1 What is the scientific name for the bone commonly referred to as the ankle?

2 Who was the original lead singer with heavy rock band Black Sabbath?

3 On a British Monopoly board which is the first property you reach after passing 'GO'?

4 Which chemical element has the symbol Ca?

TEAM B

1 What is the scientific name for the bone commonly referred to as the thigh bone?

2 Who was the original lead singer with heavy rock band Deep Purple?

3 On a British Monopoly board which is the last property you pass before reaching 'GO'?

4 Which chemical element has the symbol Co?

Answers

1 Talus

2 Ozzy Osborne.

3 Old Kent Road.

4 Calcium.

1 Femur.

2 Ian Gillan.

3 Mayfair.

4 Cobalt.

LEAGUE QUIZ 1
ROUND 5 – TEAM QUESTIONS

TEAM A
Questions

1 Which classic gangster film featured a character called Cody Jarrett?

2 Which large desert is situated in Botswana?

3 What does the place name suffix 'BURN' signify (eg Blackburn)?

4 On which famous horse did Walter Swinburn win the 1981 English Derby?

TEAM B

1 Which classic gangster film featured a character called Enrico Bandello?

2 Which large desert is situated in Chile?

3 What does the place name suffix 'KIRK' signify (eg Selkirk)?

4 On which famous horse did Bob Champion win the 1981 English Grand National?

Answers

1 *White Heat*.

2 Kalahari.

3 'Stream'.

4 Shergar.

1 *Little Caesar*.

2 Atacama.

3 'Church'.

4 Aldaniti.

LEAGUE QUIZ 1
ROUND 6 – TEAM QUESTIONS

TEAM A
Questions

1 Which river does the German city of Cologne stand on?

2 In children's cartoons, whom does Sylvester chase?

3 Who was the taxi driver who became Mastermind champion?

4 Henry Williamson wrote several books with a creature as the central character. What type of creature was Salar?

TEAM B

1 Which river does the French city of Lyons stand on?

2 In children's cartoons, whom does Wile E Coyote chase?

3 Who was the train driver who became Mastermind champion?

4 Henry Williamson wrote several books with a creature as the central character. What type of creature was Shardik?

Answers

1 River Rhine.

2 Tweety Pie.

3 Fred Housego.

4 A salmon.

1 River Rhône.

2 Road Runner.

3 Christopher Hughes.

4 A bear.

LEAGUE QUIZ 1
ROUND 7 – INDIVIDUAL QUESTIONS

TEAM A
Questions

1 A lack of which vitamin can cause the disease rickets?

2 In the Bible what was the name of the man whom Jesus brought back to life?

3 Who was the supreme god of Greek mythology?

4 In Britain they are known as curtains. What are they called in the USA?

TEAM B

1 A lack of which vitamin can cause the disease beriberi?

2 In the Bible what was the name of the robber who was released instead of Jesus?

3 Who was the supreme god of Norse mythology?

4 In Britain it is called a spanner. What do they call it in the USA?

Answers

1 Vitamin D.

2 Lazarus.

3 Zeus.

4 Drapes.

1 Vitamin B.

2 Barabbas.

3 Odin.

4 A wrench.

LEAGUE QUIZ 1
ROUND 8 – TEAM QUESTIONS

TEAM A
Questions

1 What does the letter 'P' stand for in the acronym OPEC?

2 Which American city's football team is called 'The Steelers'?

3 'The better part of valour is discretion'. From which Shakespearian play does this well known phrase come?

4 Which word can precede all of the following words? Bath, bank, brother.

TEAM B

1 What does the letter 'L' stand for in the acronym SALT?

2 Which American city's football team is called 'The Broncos'?

3 'The course of true love never did run smooth'. From which Shakespearian play does this well known phrase come?

4 Which word can precede all of the following words? Bed, wheel, cannon.

Answers

1 'Petroleum'.
Stands for: 'Organisation of Petroleum Exporting Countries'.

2 Pittsburgh.

3 *King Henry IV, Part One.*

4 Blood.

1 'Limitation'.
Stands for: 'Strategic Arms Limitation Talks'.

2 Denver.

3 *A Midsummer Night's Dream.*

4 Water.

LEAGUE QUIZ 2

ROUND 1 – TEAM QUESTIONS

TEAM A
Questions

1 Which famous American said 'I have a dream'?

2 Which organ of the body is made up of left and right ventricles and auricles?

3 Of which Australian state is Sydney the capital?

4 What was the first name of Mr Sedgman, the 1952 men's Wimbledon champion?

TEAM B

1 Which famous American said 'I am the greatest'?

2 Which organ of the body is made up of parietal, frontal, temporal and occipital lobes?

3 Of which Australian state is Melbourne the capital?

4 What was the first name of Mr Cooper, the 1958 men's Wimbledon champion?

Answers

1 Martin Luther King.

2 The heart.

3 New South Wales.

4 Frank.

1 Muhammad Ali (Cassius Clay).

2 The brain.

3 Victoria.

4 Ashley.

LEAGUE QUIZ 2
ROUND 2 – TEAM QUESTIONS

TEAM A
Questions
1 Which country fought a civil war between the years 1642–1646?

2 In a medieval castle, what name was given to the iron gate that was lifted vertically to allow entry?

3 Which of the twelve disciples of Jesus denied knowing him three times?

4 Hegel, Bentham, Wittgenstein. All are well known names in which particular field?

TEAM B
1 Which country fought a civil war between the years 1861–1865?

2 In a medieval castle, what name was given to the tower situated near the entrance gate and drawbridge?

3 Which of the twelve disciples of Jesus did not believe that he would be resurrected?

4 Newton, Leibnitz, Napier. All are well known names in which particular field?

Answers
1 England.

2 The portcullis.

3 Peter.

4 Philosophy.

1 The USA.

2 The barbican.

3 Thomas (Doubting Thomas).

4 Mathematics.

LEAGUE QUIZ 2
ROUND 3 – INDIVIDUAL QUESTIONS

TEAM A
Questions

1 What do Americans call what we call an estate car?

2 Which famous character had a housekeeper called Mrs Hudson?

3 Which artist painted *The Night Watch*?

4 Which planet in our solar system orbits the sun in the shortest time?

TEAM B

1 What do Americans call what we call a tram?

2 Which television family had a butler called Mr Hudson?

3 Which artist painted *Sunflowers*?

4 What planet in our solar system takes the longest time to orbit the sun?

Answers

1 Station wagon.

2 Sherlock Holmes.

3 Rembrandt.

4 Mercury (88 days).

1 Streetcar.

2 The Bellamy family (in *Upstairs Downstairs*).

3 Van Gogh.

4 Pluto (247.7 years!!).

LEAGUE QUIZ 2
ROUND 4 – TEAM QUESTIONS

TEAM A
Questions

1 In which city is the famous Guggenheim museum?

2 In which film did the character Popeye Doyle make his screen debut?

3 Who composed '*The New World*' *Symphony*?

4 Name the effeminate salesman in the television comedy series *Are You Being Served*?

TEAM B

1 In which city is the famous Hermitage museum?

2 In which film did the character Eddie Felson make his screen debut?

3 Who composed '*The Clock*' *Symphony*?

4 Name the senior lady assistant in the television comedy series *Are You Being Served*?

Answers

1 New York.

2 *The French Connection* (played by Gene Hackman).

3 Antonin Dvořák.

4 Mr Humphries (played by John Inman).

1 St Petersburg.

2 *The Hustler* (played by Paul Newman).

3 (Franz) Joseph Haydn.

4 Mrs Slocombe (played by Mollie Sugden).

LEAGUE QUIZ 2
ROUND 5 – TEAM QUESTIONS

TEAM A
Questions

1 The city of Buffalo in the USA stands on the shore of which of the Great Lakes?

2 Which singer was backed by *The Mindbenders*?

3 The larva of the boll-weevil is highly destructive to which plant?

4 Who was the first boxer to defeat Frank Bruno in his professional career?

TEAM B

1 The city of Milwaukee in the USA stands on the shore of which of the Great Lakes?

2 Which singer was backed by *The Attractions*?

3 The larva of the Colorado beetle is highly destructive to which plant?

4 Who did Frank Bruno first challenge for the World Heavyweight boxing title?

Answers

1 Lake Erie.

2 Wayne Fontana.

3 The cotton plant.

4 James Smith.

1 Lake Michigan.

2 Elvis Costello.

3 The potato plant.

4 Tim Witherspoon.

LEAGUE QUIZ 2
ROUND 6 – TEAM QUESTIONS

TEAM A
Questions

1 Who said in 1989:
'Frankly I wish I had
written a more critical
book'?

2 Which particular place
name is associated with
Saint Francis?

3 Which foodstuff has a
name which literally
means 'baked twice'?

4 Which famous writer
caused a mystery by
disappearing for a few
weeks in 1926?

TEAM B

1 Who said in 1990:
'I am still at the crease
though the bowling has
been more hostile
lately'?

2 Which particular place
name is associated with
Mother Theresa?

3 Which food has a name
which literally means 'on
a skewer'?

4 Which famous writer
used to work at Warren's
Boot Blacking Factory as
a boy?

Answers

1 Salman Rushdie (about his
novel *The Satanic Verses*).

2 Assisi.

3 Biscuit.

4 Agatha Christie.

1 Margaret Thatcher (shortly
before she was replaced as
Conservative Party leader).

2 Calcutta.

3 Kebab.

4 Charles Dickens.

LEAGUE QUIZ 2
ROUND 7 – INDIVIDUAL QUESTIONS

TEAM A

Questions

1 Who was killed in a speed boat accident on Coniston Water in 1967?

2 The IAAF is the governing body of which sport?

3 What is 15% of 20?

4 What type of creature is an ibex?

TEAM B

1 Who was killed in a car crash in California in September 1955?

2 The ITF is the governing body of which sport?

3 What is 30% of 40?

4 What type of creature is an ibis?

Answers

1 Donald Campbell.

2 Athletics.

3 3.

4 A horned mountain goat.

1 James Dean.

2 Tennis.

3 12.

4 A wading bird.

LEAGUE QUIZ 2
ROUND 8 – TEAM QUESTIONS

TEAM A
Questions

1 What name is given to a male duck?

2 Who wrote the famous poem *The Pied Piper of Hamelin*?

3 What is the capital city of the Italian region of Tuscany?

4 Which organisation has the motto 'Nation shall speak peace unto nation'?

TEAM B

1 What name is given to a male goose?

2 Who wrote the famous poem *The Charge of the Light Brigade*?

3 What is the capital city of the Italian region of Piedmont?

4 Which organisation has the motto 'Let not the deep swallow me up'?

Answers

1 A drake.

2 Robert Browning.

3 Florence.

4 The BBC.

1 A gander.

2 Alfred Tennyson.

3 Turin.

4 The Royal National Lifeboat Institution.

LEAGUE QUIZ 3
ROUND 1 – TEAM QUESTIONS

TEAM A
Questions

1 By what name was film star Frances Gumm better known?

2 Where in Italy is the Bridge of Sighs?

3 What type of farm creature is a Tamworth?

4 Who was on the British throne at the time of the Great Fire of London?

TEAM B

1 By what name was film star Marion Morrison better known?

2 Where in Italy is the Uffizi Gallery?

3 What type of farm creature is a Rhode Island Red?

4 Which British King was on the throne at the time of the Gunpowder Plot?

Answers

1 Judy Garland.

2 Venice.

3 Pig.

4 Charles II.

1 John Wayne.

2 Florence.

3 Chicken.

4 James I (James VI of Scotland).

LEAGUE QUIZ 3
ROUND 2 – TEAM QUESTIONS

TEAM A
Questions

1 What colour is the gemstone emerald?

2 Whom did Steve Davis defeat to win the 1981 World Snooker Championship?

3 What name is given to the Japanese art of paper folding?

4 Who on television had a 'Frame Game'?

TEAM B

1 What colour is the gemstone sapphire?

2 Whom did Steve Davis defeat to win the 1988 World Snooker Championship?

3 What name is given to the art of beautiful handwriting?

4 Who on television had a 'Full House'?

Answers

1 Green.

2 Doug Mountjoy.

3 Origami.

4 Jimmy Tarbuck.

1 Blue. (It is possible to have different colours, but they are not recognised as being gemstones.)

2 Terry Griffiths.

3 Calligraphy.

4 Bob Monkhouse.

LEAGUE QUIZ 3
ROUND 3 – INDIVIDUAL QUESTIONS

TEAM A
Questions

1 What is the chemical symbol for lead?

2 In which sport is the Lance Todd trophy awarded?

3 Who won an Oscar for his portrayal of an alcoholic in the film *The Lost Weekend*?

4 What is the capital city of Syria?

TEAM B

1 What is the chemical symbol for tin?

2 In which sport is the Ritz Club Trophy awarded?

3 Who won an Oscar for his portrayal of a hypocritical evangelist in the film *Elmer Gantry*?

4 What is the capital city of Jordan?

Answers

1 Pb (from plumbum).

2 Rugby league.

3 Ray Milland.

4 Damascus.

1 Sn (from stannum).

2 Horse racing.

3 Burt Lancaster.

4 Amman.

LEAGUE QUIZ 3
ROUND 4 – TEAM QUESTIONS

TEAM A
Questions

1 At which horse racing venue can you see 'Tattenham Corner'?

2 Which well known children's character was created by Michael Bond?

3 What is the name of the alloy made from tin and lead?

4 Which group had a number one hit in 1970 with a song called *Yellow River*?

TEAM B

1 At which cricketing venue can you see 'The Hill'?

2 Which well known children's character was created by Eric Hill?

3 What is the name of the alloy made from copper and zinc?

4 Which group had a number one hit in 1972 with a song called *Son of my Father*?

Answers

1 Epsom racecourse.

2 Paddington Bear.

3 Pewter.

4 Christie.

1 Sydney cricket ground.

2 Spot the Dog.

3 Brass.

4 Chicory Tip.

LEAGUE QUIZ 3
ROUND 5 – TEAM QUESTIONS

TEAM A

Questions

1 In the early episodes of the TV soap *Coronation Street*, what was the favourite drink of Ena Sharples?

2 What would you have to do to win an Edgar?

3 Which drug has a name derived from the name of the Roman God of Sleep and Dreams?

4 What is the name of the famous spectral ship said to haunt the Cape of Good Hope?

TEAM B

1 In the early episodes of the TV soap *Coronation Street*, what was the name of the cat owned by Minnie Caldwell?

2 What would you have to do to win the Bollingen Prize?

3 Which geographical feature derives its name from the Roman God of Fire?

4 What was the name of the famous ship sunk in 1545 and raised in 1982?

Answers

1 Milk stout.

2 Write a book. (The Edgar is awarded annually in the USA to the best mystery novel.)

3 Morphine (from Morpheus).

4 *Flying Dutchman.*

1 Bobbie.

2 Write some poetry. (It is awarded annually for the best American poetry.)

3 Volcano (from Vulcan).

4 *Mary Rose.*

LEAGUE QUIZ 3
ROUND 6 – TEAM QUESTIONS

TEAM A
Questions

1 Which one word can have the following two meanings?
   a) A preliminary sketch.
   b) To conscript for military service.

2 The enormous sequoia tree of North America has a much better known name. What is it?

3 Which is the lowest of the five ranks of the peerage in Britain?

4 Miranda and Prospero are both characters from which of Shakespeare's plays?

TEAM B

1 Which one word can have the following two meanings?
   a) A long piece of timber.
   b) A collection of parallel rays.

2 The Norwegian spruce tree has a much better known name. What is it?

3 Which is the highest of the five ranks of the peerage in Britain?

4 Bassanio and Antonio are both characters from which of Shakespeare's plays?

Answers

1 Draft.

2 Giant Redwood.

3 Baron.

4 *The Tempest*.

1 Beam.

2 Christmas tree.

3 Duke.

4 *The Merchant of Venice*.

LEAGUE QUIZ 3
ROUND 7 – INDIVIDUAL QUESTIONS

TEAM A
Questions

1 How many contestants took part in each programme of the TV show *Bullseye*?

2 Which creatures are kept in an apiary?

3 The Volkswagen Beetle was designed in the 1930s by which famous car designer?

4 Where do Scotland play home international rugby union matches?

TEAM B

1 How many contestants took part in each programme of the TV show *Mastermind*?

2 Which creatures live in a home called a holt?

3 The Austin Mini was designed in the 1950s by which famous car designer?

4 Where do Ireland play home international rugby union matches?

Answers

1 Six.

2 Bees.

3 Ferdinand Porsche.

4 Murrayfield [Edinburgh].

1 Four.

2 Otters.

3 Alec Issigonis.

4 Lansdowne Road [Dublin].

LEAGUE QUIZ 3
ROUND 8 – TEAM QUESTIONS

TEAM A
Questions

1 Which musical instrument was played by band leader Glenn Miller?

2 The national flag of the Republic of Ireland is composed of three colours. White, green and which other colour?

3 According to their adverts, which is the bank that 'likes to say yes'?

4 Who painted *Girl Before a Mirror*?

TEAM B

1 Which musical instrument was played by band leader Benny Goodman?

2 The national flag of Belgium is composed of three colours. Black, red and which other colour?

3 According to their adverts, which bank is the 'listening bank'?

4 Who painted *Girl Reading a Letter*?

Answers

1 Trombone.

2 Orange.

3 Trustee Savings Bank (TSB).

4 Pablo Picasso.

1 Clarinet.

2 Yellow.

3 Midland Bank.

4 Jan Vermeer.

LEAGUE QUIZ 4

ROUND 1 – TEAM QUESTIONS

TEAM A
Questions

1 Who in the Bible was cast into the lions' den?

2 Bob Hewitt was one half of a famous tennis doubles pair who were Wimbledon doubles champions in 1967, 1972 and 1978. Who was his partner?

3 *Sebhorric dermatitis* is the correct name of which common minor bodily affliction?

4 What was the name of the *Addams Family* character played in the original TV series by John Astin?

TEAM B

1 Who in the Bible wore a coat of many colours?

2 John Newcombe was one half of a famous tennis pairing who were Wimbledon doubles champions in 1968, 1969 and 1970. Who was his partner?

3 *Tinea pedis* is the correct name of which common minor bodily affliction?

4 What was the name of the *Addams Family* character played in the original TV series by Carolyn Jones?

Answers

1 Daniel.

2 Frew McMillan.

3 Dandruff.

4 Gomez.

1 Joseph.

2 Tony Roche.

3 Athlete's foot.

4 Morticia.

LEAGUE QUIZ 4
ROUND 2 – TEAM QUESTIONS

TEAM A
Questions

1 Which well known children's story opens with the line 'All children except one grow up'?

2 In which year of the 1950s was the British steel industry nationalised for the first time?

3 Carson City is the capital of which American state?

4 Who was the voice of cartoon character Bugs Bunny?

TEAM B

1 Which well known nautical story opens with the line 'Call me Ishmael'?

2 In which year of the 1960s was the British steel industry nationalised for the second time?

3 Jefferson City is the capital of which American state?

4 Who was the voice of cartoon character Donald Duck?

Answers

1 *Peter Pan*.

2 1951 (January 1st).

3 Nevada.

4 Mel Blanc.

1 *Moby Dick*.

2 1967 (July 28th).

3 Missouri.

4 Clarence Nash.

LEAGUE QUIZ 4
ROUND 3 – INDIVIDUAL QUESTIONS

TEAM A
Questions

1 *Coalminer's Daughter* was the title of a film concerning the life of which singer?

2 What nationality was the explorer Ferdinand Magellan?

3 What kind of transport is an ACV?

4 Which fish has a name that is also the slang term for fingerprint?

TEAM B

1 *Funny Girl* was the title of a film concerning the life of which entertainer?

2 What nationality was the explorer Abel Tasman?

3 What kind of transport is an AFV?

4 Which fish has a name that is also one of the positions used in diving?

Answers

1 Loretta Lynn.

2 Portuguese.

3 A hovercraft (Air Cushioned Vehicle).

4 A dab.

1 Fanny Brice.

2 Dutch.

3 A tank (Armoured Fighting Vehicle).

4 A pike.

LEAGUE QUIZ 4
ROUND 4 – TEAM QUESTIONS

TEAM A

Questions

1 Which of the seven wonders of the ancient world was situated at Rhodes?

2 Which particular commodity is associated with Hatton Garden in London?

3 What name is given to the scientific study of animals?

4 Within one year, in which year was the last man executed in Britain?

TEAM B

1 Which of the seven wonders of the ancient world was situated at Babylon?

2 Which particular commodity is associated with Mincing Lane in London?

3 What name is given to the scientific study of plants?

4 Within one year, in which year was the last woman executed in Britain?

Answers

1 The Colossus.

2 Diamonds.

3 Zoology.

4 1964 (Peter Allen and John Walby).

1 The Hanging Gardens.

2 Tea.

3 Botany.

4 1955 (Ruth Ellis).

LEAGUE QUIZ 4
ROUND 5 – TEAM QUESTIONS

TEAM A
Questions
1 Which 1980s pop group included the Kemp brothers in their line up?

2 What is the connection between Asa Hartford, John Denver and Dusty Springfield?

3 What is measured using an instrument called a barometer?

4 Who was Britain's 1976 World Motor Racing Champion?

TEAM B

1 Which 1980s pop group included the Pearson brothers in their line up?

2 What is the connection between British Columbia, Hong Kong and The Seychelles?

3 What is measured using an instrument called a micrometer?

4 Who was Britain's 1976 World Motor Cycling Champion?

Answers
1 Spandau Ballet.

2 All their surnames are state capitals in the USA.

3 Atmospheric pressure.

4 James Hunt.

1 Five Star.

2 All have a capital city called Victoria.

3 Small distances.

4 Barry Sheene.

LEAGUE QUIZ 4
ROUND 6 – TEAM QUESTIONS

TEAM A
Questions

1 The word 'BUS', being a type of public transport, is a shortened version of which other word?

2 Name one of the two breeds of dog that are generally accepted as being the world's smallest breeds.

3 Who was the famous leader of the Desert Rats during World War II?

4 In which month does the annual event of the Lord Mayor's Show take place in London?

TEAM B

1 The word 'CAB', being a type of public transport, is a shortened version of which other word?

2 Name one of the two breeds of dog that are generally accepted as being the world's tallest breeds.

3 Which German Field Marshal of World War II was nicknamed 'The Desert Fox'?

4 In which month does the annual event of the Last Night of the Proms take place at the Royal Albert Hall?

Answers

1 Omnibus.

2 Yorkshire Terrier or Chihuahua.

3 Field Marshal Bernard Law Montgomery.

4 November.

1 Cabriolet.

2 Irish Wolfhound or Great Dane.

3 Erwin Rommel.

4 September.

LEAGUE QUIZ 4
ROUND 7 – INDIVIDUAL QUESTIONS

TEAM A
Questions

1 Which famous jazz musician was nicknamed 'Duke'?

2 Which town or city was the venue on the first occasion of the Summer Olympic Games being held in the USA?

3 Which is furthest east of these cities: Nottingham, Portsmouth, Oxford, Northampton?

4 Which planet in our solar system is sometimes referred to as the 'The Red Planet'?

TEAM B

1 Which famous jazz musician was nicknamed 'Count'?

2 Which town or city was the venue on the first occasion of the Winter Olympic Games being held in the USA?

3 Which is furthest east of these cities: Edinburgh, Bristol, Liverpool, Cardiff?

4 Which planet in our solar system is sometimes referred to as 'The Evening Star'?

Answers

1 Edward Ellington.

2 St Louis in 1904.

3 Northampton.

4 Mars.

1 William Basie.

2 Lake Placid in 1932.

3 Bristol.

4 Venus.

LEAGUE QUIZ 4
ROUND 8 – TEAM QUESTIONS

TEAM A
Questions

1 What is the name of the computer featured on the TV quiz show *Family Fortunes*?

2 What name was given to the type of art particularly associated with Salvador Dali?

3 Which president of the USA had the middle name David?

4 How many characters are there in the Russian alphabet?

TEAM B

1 What is the name of the computer-generated character featured on the TV quiz show *Catchphrase*?

2 What name was given to the type of art particularly associated with Jackson Pollock?

3 Which president of the USA had the middle name Baines?

4 How many characters are there in the Greek alphabet?

Answers

1 Mr Babbage.

2 Surrealism.

3 Dwight D Eisenhower.

4 33.

1 Mr Chips.

2 Abstract expressionism (or action painting).

3 Lyndon B Johnson.

4 24.

LEAGUE QUIZ 5
ROUND 1 – TEAM QUESTIONS

TEAM A
Questions

1 Where could you see four sculptures by Gutzon Borglum in close proximity in the USA?

2 Whose is the first birth recorded in the Bible?

3 Which TV cop used the catchphrase 'Book 'em Danno'?

4 The Scottish chemist who invented and patented a waterproof fabric died in 1843. Who was he?

TEAM B

1 Where could you see four sculptures by Edwin Landseer in close proximity in the UK?

2 For what was the biblical King Solomon renowned?

3 Which TV cop used the catchphrase 'Who loves ya baby'?

4 The Scottish inventor of the modern system of road surfacing died in 1836. Who was he?

Answers

1 Mount Rushmore. (Borglum sculpted the four US presidents' heads that can be seen at Mount Rushmore.)

2 Cain's.

3 Steve McGarrett (played by Jack Lord in *Hawaii Five 0*).

4 Charles Mackintosh.

1 Trafalgar Square. (Landseer sculpted the four lions at the base of Nelson's Column.)

2 His wisdom.

3 Theo Kojak (played by Telly Savalas in *Kojak*).

4 John Macadam.

LEAGUE QUIZ 5
ROUND 2 – TEAM QUESTIONS

TEAM A
Questions

1 Otology is a medical speciality dealing with which part of the body?

2 What is the name of the fictional detective created by Harry Blyth?

3 Which city is home to superhero Batman?

4 Who in mythology killed the Gorgon Medusa?

TEAM B

1 Rhinology is a medical condition dealing with which part of the body?

2 What is the name of the fictional detective created by Chester Gould?

3 Which city is home to superhero Superman?

4 Who in mythology killed the Minotaur?

Answers

1 The ear.

2 Sexton Blake.

3 Gotham City.

4 Perseus.

1 The nose.

2 Dick Tracy.

3 Metropolis.

4 Theseus.

LEAGUE QUIZ 5
ROUND 3 – INDIVIDUAL QUESTIONS

TEAM A
Questions

1 Which American city is known as The Windy City?

2 Which animal has a name that means 'Earth Pig' in English?

3 Which famous sports car company was founded by Colin Chapman?

4 Which country lies between Austria and Switzerland?

TEAM B

1 Which American city is known as Motor City?

2 Which animal has a name that means 'No Drink' in English?

3 Which famous sports car company was founded by William Lyons?

4 Which country lies between Spain and France?

Answers

1 Chicago.

2 Aardvark.

3 Lotus.

4 Liechtenstein.

1 Detroit.

2 Koala.

3 Jaguar.

4 Andorra.

LEAGUE QUIZ 5
ROUND 4 – TEAM QUESTIONS

TEAM A
Questions

1 Which letter, apart from the letter X, scores 8 points in the game of *Scrabble*?

2 *Angie* by The Rolling Stones was a tribute to whom?

3 Virgil Tibbs was the name of a policeman character in which original classic film?

4 According to the children's rhyme *Oranges and Lemons*, which bell said 'You owe me five farthings'?

TEAM B

1 Which letter scores 5 points in the game of *Scrabble*?

2 *O Carol* by Neil Sedaka was a tribute to whom?

3 Tom Powers was the name of a gangster character in which classic film?

4 According to the children's rhyme *Oranges and Lemons*, which bell said 'When I grow rich'?

Answers

1 The letter J.

2 Angie Bowie.

3 *In the Heat of the Night* (there were two sequels).

4 St Martin's.

1 The letter K.

2 Carole King.

3 *Public Enemy*.

4 Shoreditch.

LEAGUE QUIZ 5
ROUND 5 – TEAM QUESTIONS

TEAM A
Questions

1 Which player was unfortunate enough to score for both teams in the 1987 FA Cup final?

2 Which well known musical film is based on a book called *Green Grow the Rushes*?

3 In which year did man first reach the summit of Mount Everest?

4 Which two countries share a border with Sweden?

TEAM B

1 Which player was unfortunate enough to miss a penalty in the 1988 FA Cup final?

2 Which well known musical film is based on a book called *Sobbin' Women*?

3 In which year was the Berlin Wall erected?

4 Which two countries share a border with Uruguay?

Answers

1 Gary Mabbutt (Spurs v Coventry).

2 *Oklahoma!*

3 1953.

4 Finland and Norway.

1 John Aldridge (Liverpool v Wimbledon).

2 *Seven Brides for Seven Brothers*.

3 1961.

4 Argentina and Brazil.

LEAGUE QUIZ 5
ROUND 6 – TEAM QUESTIONS

TEAM A
Questions

1 How long (approximately) does it take for the earth to revolve on its own axis once?

2 Which famous English poet died of tuberculosis in Rome in 1821?

3 Which is the only mammal capable of true flight?

4 Which was the first book to feature the character James Bond?

TEAM B

1 How long (approximately) does it take for the earth to orbit the sun once?

2 Which famous English poet drowned while sailing near Spezia in Italy in 1822?

3 Which is the only bird that can fly backwards?

4 Which was the first book to feature the character Sherlock Holmes?

Answers

1 24 hours.

2 John Keats.

3 The bat.

4 *Casino Royale*.

1 1 year.

2 Percy Shelley.

3 The hummingbird.

4 *A Study in Scarlet*.

LEAGUE QUIZ 5

ROUND 7 – INDIVIDUAL QUESTIONS

TEAM A
Questions

1 Which Conservative politician was given the nickname 'Goldilocks', among others, during the 1980s?

2 In a literary title how were the characters Mrs Page and Mrs Ford better known?

3 Who is associated with the equation $E = mc^2$?

4 Who is the traditional patron saint of travellers?

TEAM B

1 Which Labour politician became nicknamed 'The Beast of Bolsover' during the 1980s?

2 In a literary title how were the characters Valentine and Proteus better known?

3 Who discovered the law of gravity?

4 Who is the traditional patron saint of children?

Answers

1 Michael Heseltine.

2 *The Merry Wives of Windsor*.

3 Albert Einstein.

4 Saint Christopher.

1 Dennis Skinner.

2 *Two Gentlemen of Verona*.

3 Isaac Newton.

4 Saint Nicholas.

LEAGUE QUIZ 5
ROUND 8 – TEAM QUESTIONS

TEAM A
Questions

1 Which type of hat was worn by Sherlock Holmes?

2 World War II. Which country surrendered on 28th September 1942?

3 Which word describes a native of the city of Plymouth?

4 In which 1982 film did Julie Andrews dress up as a man?

TEAM B

1 Which type of hat is named after a country?

2 World War II. Which country was invaded by Operation Barbarossa?

3 Which word describes a native of the city of Newcastle? (NOT Geordie.)

4 In which 1982 film did Dustin Hoffman dress up as a woman?

Answers

1 Deerstalker.

2 Italy.

3 Plymothian.

4 *Victor/Victoria*.

1 Panama.

2 Russia (by Germany).

3 Novocastrian.

4 *Tootsie*.

LEAGUE QUIZ 6
ROUND 1 – TEAM QUESTIONS

TEAM A
Questions

1 Which book features a parrot called Polynesia?

2 Which Latin phrase means without limit, continuing for ever?

3 The first animal in space was a dog called Laika. What was the name of the spacecraft that put it there?

4 According to legend, where was the court of King Arthur?

TEAM B

1 Which book features a parrot called Captain Flint?

2 Which Latin phrase means to excess, to a sickening degree?

3 The first man in space was the Russian cosmonaut Yuri Gagarin. What was the name of the spacecraft that put him there?

4 According to legend, what was the name of the sword pulled from the stone by King Arthur?

Answers

1 *Dr Dolittle* (by Hugh Lofting).

2 Ad infinitum.

3 Sputnik II.

4 Camelot.

1 *Treasure Island* (by Robert Louis Stevenson).

2 Ad nauseam.

3 Vostok I.

4 Excalibur.

LEAGUE QUIZ 6
ROUND 2 – TEAM QUESTIONS

TEAM A
Questions

1 Who in the Bible had sons named Ishmael and Isaac?

2 What was the name of the character played by David Jason in the TV show *Open All Hours*?

3 What was the name of the ship that took the Pilgrim Fathers to America?

4 The Celsius scale of temperature is named after Anders Celsius. What was his nationality?

TEAM B

1 Who in the Bible had sons named Solomon and Absalom?

2 What was the name of the character played by David Jason in the TV show *Porterhouse Blue*?

3 Who was the most famous captain of the *Golden Hind*?

4 The Fahrenheit scale of temperature is named after Gabriel Fahrenheit. What was his nationality?

Answers

1 Abraham.

2 Granville.

3 *Mayflower*.

4 Swedish.

1 David.

2 Skullion.

3 Sir Francis Drake.

4 German.

LEAGUE QUIZ 6
ROUND 3 – INDIVIDUAL QUESTIONS

TEAM A
Questions

1 Which actor played the part of King Henry VIII in the film *A Man for all Seasons*?

2 The 'Goldwing' is a famous make of motorcycle produced by which company?

3 What name is given to the national flag of France?

4 Which is the only play by William Shakespeare with the name of an animal in the title?

TEAM B

1 Which actor played the part of King Henry VIII in the film *Anne of the Thousand Days*?

2 The 'Electraglide' is a famous make of motorcycle produced by which company?

3 What name is given to the personal flag of the sovereign of Great Britain?

4 Which is the only play by William Shakespeare with a British place name in the title?

Answers

1 Robert Shaw.

2 Honda.

3 Tricolour.

4 *The Taming of the Shrew.*

1 Richard Burton.

2 Harley Davidson.

3 Royal Standard.

4 *The Merry Wives of Windsor.*

LEAGUE QUIZ 6
ROUND 4 – TEAM QUESTIONS

TEAM A
Questions

1 Name one of the two countries in which you could find people known as Tamils.

2 *Everything I Own* was a hit in 1974 for Ken Boothe. Who had a hit with the same song in 1987?

3 What type of creature is a Kodiak?

4 The age of a fish can be determined by examining which part of its anatomy?

TEAM B

1 Name one of the two countries in which you could find people known as Masai.

2 *Always on My Mind* was a hit in 1972 for Elvis Presley. Who had a hit with the same song in 1987?

3 What type of creature is a Pronghorn?

4 The age of a horse can be determined by examining which part of its anatomy?

Answers

1 India or Sri Lanka.

2 Boy George.

3 A bear.

4 Scales.

1 Kenya or Tanzania.

2 Pet Shop Boys.

3 An antelope.

4 Teeth.

LEAGUE QUIZ 6

ROUND 5 – TEAM QUESTIONS

TEAM A
Questions

1 Which team game was devised by William Morgan in Massachusetts in 1895?

2 In the film of the same name, what was the Love Bug?

3 Which drink is sometimes referred to as 'Adam's Ale'?

4 In which well known TV show could you have been served a drink by Amos Brearley?

TEAM B

1 Which team game was devised by Dr. James Naismith in Massachusetts in 1891?

2 In the film of the same name, what was the *African Queen*?

3 Which drink is sometimes referred to as 'Mother's Ruin'?

4 In which well known TV show could you have been served a drink by Gloria Todd?

Answers

1 Volleyball.

2 A Volkswagen Beetle Car (called Herbie).

3 Water.

4 *Emmerdale Farm* (at the Woolpack Inn).

1 Basketball.

2 A river boat.

3 Gin.

4 *Coronation Street* (at the Rovers Return).

LEAGUE QUIZ 6
ROUND 6 – TEAM QUESTIONS

TEAM A
Questions

1 What is the name of the Indian clay oven used to grill food?

2 Psychologists may sometimes refer to the initials 'ESP'. What do they stand for?

3 Who in the world of cricket was known as 'The Gnome'?

4 The region of Flanders was the site of fierce fighting during World War I. In which country is it situated?

TEAM B

1 What is the name of the large frying pan used to prepare Chinese food?

2 Psychologists may sometimes refer to the initials 'REM'. What do they stand for?

3 Who in the world of snooker was known as 'The Grinder'?

4 The town of Arnhem was the site of fierce fighting during World War II. In which country is it situated?

Answers

1 A tandoor.

2 Extra Sensory Perception.

3 Keith Fletcher.

4 Belgium.

1 A wok.

2 Rapid Eye Movement (when dreaming).

3 Cliff Thorburn.

4 The Netherlands.

LEAGUE QUIZ 6
ROUND 7 – INDIVIDUAL QUESTIONS

TEAM A

Questions

1 Common salt is composed of equal amounts of sodium and which other chemical element?

2 To which animal family does the chipmunk belong?

3 Supply the missing word to complete this proverb. '------ is nine tenths of the law'.

4 Who was the first man to beat Eric Bristow in the final of the World Darts Championships?

TEAM B

1 By volume, what is the principal chemical element contained in rain water?

2 To which animal family does the llama belong?

3 Supply the missing word to complete this proverb. '------ is the spice of life'.

4 Who was the first man to beat Steve Davis in the final of the World Snooker Championships?

Answers

1 Chlorine.

2 Squirrel.

3 Possession.

4 Keith Deller.

1 Hydrogen.

2 Camel.

3 Variety.

4 Dennis Taylor.

LEAGUE QUIZ 6
ROUND 8 – TEAM QUESTIONS

TEAM A
Questions

1 What is the speciality of the publishing company Haynes?

2 What was the name of the eagle that twice escaped from London Zoo in 1965?

3 Who created the character of Professor Van Helsing?

4 Who was the first man to win one hundred England caps for soccer?

TEAM B

1 What is the speciality of the publishing company Bartholomews?

2 What was the name of the panda that was flown to Moscow from London Zoo in 1966?

3 Who created the character of Professor Moriarty?

4 Who was the first man to win one hundred England caps for cricket?

Answers

1 Car manuals.

2 Goldie.

3 Bram Stoker in *Dracula*.

4 Billy Wright.

1 Maps (or atlases).

2 Chi Chi.

3 Sir Arthur Conan Doyle in the *Sherlock Holmes* stories.

4 Colin Cowdrey.

LEAGUE QUIZ 7
ROUND 1 – TEAM QUESTIONS

TEAM A
Questions

TEAM B

1 Which British prime minister is associated with the phrase 'Never was so much owed by so many to so few'?

1 Which British prime minister is associated with the phrase 'You never had it so good'?

2 Which country stages a motor racing Grand Prix at Monza?

2 Which country stages a motor racing Grand Prix at Spa?

3 Ibiza is a part of which group of holiday islands?

3 Lanzarote is part of which group of holiday islands?

4 In Greek mythology, how many Gorgons were there?

4 In Greek mythology, how many Muses were there?

Answers

1 Winston Churchill.

1 Harold Macmillan.

2 Italy.

2 Belgium.

3 The Balearics.

3 The Canary Islands.

4 Three.

4 Nine.

LEAGUE QUIZ 7
ROUND 2 – TEAM QUESTIONS

TEAM A

Questions

1 Which American author wrote *The Old Man and the Sea*?

2 What is the US equivalent of the British FT Index?

3 Earth is the third planet from the sun in our solar system, which is the second?

4 Who had a 1957 chart hit with *Tutti Frutti*?

TEAM B

1 Which American author wrote *East of Eden*?

2 What is the Japanese equivalent of the British FT Index?

3 Earth is the third planet from the sun in our solar system, which is the fourth?

4 Who had a 1958 chart hit with *Summertime Blues*?

Answers

1 Ernest Hemingway.

2 The Dow Jones Index.

3 Venus.

4 Little Richard.

1 John Steinbeck.

2 The Nikkei Dow Index.

3 Mars.

4 Eddie Cochrane.

LEAGUE QUIZ 7
ROUND 3 – INDIVIDUAL QUESTIONS

TEAM A
Questions

1 Who won a best actor Oscar for the film *Elmer Gantry*?

2 What is the capital city of the American state of Kansas?

3 In science fiction, who was the arch enemy of Flash Gordon?

4 Who said *We Can't Dance* in the pop charts of 1992?

TEAM B

1 Who won a best actor Oscar for the film *A Man for all Seasons*?

2 What is the capital city of the American state of Texas?

3 In science fiction, who was the arch enemy of Superman?

4 Who said *Let's Stay Together* in the pop charts of 1992?

Answers

1 Burt Lancaster.

2 Topeka.

3 Ming the Merciless.

4 Genesis.

1 Paul Scofield.

2 Austin.

3 Lex Luthor.

4 The Pasadenas.

LEAGUE QUIZ 7
ROUND 4 – TEAM QUESTIONS

TEAM A
Questions

1 The Dunhill Cup is a trophy awarded in golf and named after a Mr Dunhill. What was his first name?

2 Which is the world's smallest breed of horse?

3 Which boy's name is also the name of the SI unit of inductance?

4 Which biblical character was renowned for his strength?

TEAM B

1 The Davis Cup is a trophy awarded in tennis and named after a Mr Davis. What was his first name?

2 Which is the world's smallest species of bird?

3 Which boy's name also has the dictionary definition 'to diminish slowly'?

4 Which biblical character was renowned for his patience?

Answers

1 Alfred.

2 The Falabella of Argentina.

3 Henry

4 Samson.

1 Dwight.

2 The Bee Hummingbird of Cuba.

3 Peter.

4 Job.

LEAGUE QUIZ 7
ROUND 5 – TEAM QUESTIONS

TEAM A
Questions

TEAM B

1 What, exactly, is measured with an instrument called a hydrometer?

1 What, exactly, is measured with an instrument called a manometer?

2 Which English king was known as 'The Hammer of the Scots'?

2 Which English king was known as 'The Merry Monarch'?

3 According to the well known rhyme, which day's child is 'loving and giving'?

3 According to the well known rhyme, which day's child is 'full of grace'?

4 In the television puppet show, for which organisation did the Thunderbirds work?

4 In the television puppet show, for which organisation did Captain Scarlet work?

Answers

1 Density of liquids (specific gravity).

1 Pressure of gas or liquids.

2 Edward I.

2 Charles II.

3 Friday's.

3 Tuesday's.

4 International Rescue.

4 Spectrum.

LEAGUE QUIZ 7
ROUND 6 – TEAM QUESTIONS

TEAM A
Questions

1 Which English county is particularly associated with clotted cream?

2 Which well known explorer travelled in a ship called the *Santa Maria*?

3 The adjective arboreal can be used to describe creatures that live in which particular surroundings?

4 What was the name of the horse that gave Willie Carson his first victory in the English Derby?

TEAM B

1 Which English county is particularly associated with the dish called hot pot?

2 Which well known explorer travelled in a ship called the *Endeavour*?

3 The adjective littoral can be used to describe creatures that live in which particular surroundings?

4 What was the name of the horse that gave Pat Eddery his first victory in the English Derby?

Answers

1 Devon.

2 Christopher Columbus.

3 In trees.

4 Troy in 1979.

1 Lancashire.

2 James Cook.

3 By the seashore.

4 Grundy in 1975.

LEAGUE QUIZ 7
ROUND 7 – INDIVIDUAL QUESTIONS

TEAM A
Questions

1 Which writer had the first names Pelham Grenville?

2 In general terms, what kind of food is bisque?

3 Which singer had a number one hit with *99 Red Balloons*?

4 If a dog barks and a cow moos, which creature is said to 'gibber'?

TEAM B

1 Which writer had the first names Thomas Stearns?

2 In general terms, what kind of food is pitta?

3 Which group had a number one hit with *Red Red Wine*?

4 If a dog barks and a cow moos, which creature is said to 'bell'?

Answers

1 P G Wodehouse.

2 Soup.

3 Nena.

4 An ape.

1 T S Eliot.

2 A type of flat bread.

3 UB40.

4 A deer.

LEAGUE QUIZ 7
ROUND 8 – TEAM QUESTIONS

TEAM A
Questions

1 Which flower has the scientific name *Dianthus*?

2 In which range of hills is the source of the Thames?

3 Which film of 1988 was concerned with the Great Train Robbery of the 1960s?

4 Which composer who lived 1813–1901 first achieved fame with his opera *Nabucco*?

TEAM B

1 Which flower has the scientific name *Calendula*?

2 In which range of hills is the source of the Mersey?

3 Which film of 1988 was concerned with the Profumo affair of the 1960s?

4 Which composer who lived 1792–1868 first achieved fame with his opera *Tancredi*?

Answers

1 Carnation.

2 The Cotswolds.

3 *Buster*.

4 Guiseppe Verdi.

1 Marigold.

2 The Pennines.

3 *Scandal*.

4 Gioacchino Rossini.

LEAGUE QUIZ 8
ROUND 1 – TEAM QUESTIONS

TEAM A
Questions

1 What is the chemical symbol for the element gold?

2 In 1907, who was the first British author to win the Nobel Prize for Literature?

3 Who in the Bible was the brother of Moses?

4 Who along with Vince Clark formed the pop duo Yazoo?

TEAM B

1 What is the chemical symbol for the element silver?

2 Which British author won the Nobel Prize for Literature in 1983?

3 Who in the Bible asked for the head of John the Baptist?

4 Who along with Vince Clark formed the pop duo Erasure?

Answers

1 Au (from aurum).

2 Rudyard Kipling.

3 Aaron.

4 Alison Moyet.

1 Ag (from argentum).

2 William Golding.

3 Salome.

4 Andy Bell.

LEAGUE QUIZ 8
ROUND 2 – TEAM QUESTIONS

TEAM A
Questions

1 Give both Christian and surname of the man who gave his name to the system of communication where letters are represented by dots and dashes.

2 Which team did England beat in the semi final of the 1992 World Cup of cricket?

3 Which British General was killed in Khartoum in 1885?

4 What name and number were taken by Albino Luciano when he was elected pope?

TEAM B

1 Give both Christian and surname of the man who gave his name to the system of reading for the blind where letters are represented by raised dots.

2 Which team did Pakistan beat in the semi final of the 1992 World Cup of cricket?

3 Which British General was killed near Quebec in 1759?

4 What name and number were taken by Giovanni Montini when he was elected pope?

Answers

1 Samuel Morse.

2 South Africa.

3 Charles Gordon.

4 John Paul I.

1 Louis Braille.

2 New Zealand.

3 James Wolfe.

4 Paul VI.

LEAGUE QUIZ 8
ROUND 3 – INDIVIDUAL QUESTIONS

TEAM A
Questions

1 What is the name of the type of waterproof hat worn by sailors?

2 What type of fruit is a morello?

3 Which author, better known for his spy stories, wrote *Chitty Chitty Bang Bang*?

4 In comic books and films, what is the everyday name of superhero Batman?

TEAM B

1 What name is given to the tall pointed head-dress with a cleft top worn by a bishop?

2 What type of fruit is a cantaloup?

3 Which author, better known for his detective stories, wrote *The Lost World*?

4 What is the real name of comic book and film hero Superman?

Answers

1 Sou'wester.

2 Cherry.

3 Ian Fleming

4 Bruce Wayne.

1 Mitre.

2 Melon.

3 Sir Arthur Conan Doyle.

4 Clark Kent.

LEAGUE QUIZ 8
ROUND 4 – TEAM QUESTIONS

TEAM A
Questions

1 What was the title of the first number one hit for the Beatles?

2 What is the name of the veil concealing most of the face worn by Moslem women?

3 In the books by Beatrix Potter, what kind of creature was Jeremy Fisher?

4 The region of Demerara has become associated with a type of sugar. In which South American country is Demerara?

TEAM B

1 What was the title of the first number one hit for the Rolling Stones?

2 What is the name of the long, loose robe worn by the people of Japan?

3 In the books by Beatrix Potter, what kind of creature was Mrs Tiggywinkle?

4 The town of Fray Bentos has become associated with corned beef. In which South American country is Fray Bentos?

Answers

1 *From Me To You*.

2 Yashmak.

3 A frog.

4 Guyana.

1 *It's All Over Now*.

2 Kimono.

3 A hedgehog.

4. Uruguay.

LEAGUE QUIZ 8
ROUND 5 – TEAM QUESTIONS

TEAM A
Questions

1 The English discoverer of the gas oxygen had the first name Joseph. What was his surname?

2 Who according to the Bible dwelt in the Land of Nod?

3 In which television comedy show were Peter Bowles and James Bolam hospital patients?

4 Which religious order was founded by Ignatius Loyola?

TEAM B

1 The English discoverer of the gas nitrogen had the first name Henry. What was his surname?

2 Who according to the Bible was struck blind on the road to Damascus?

3 In which television comedy show were Joan Sanderson and John Alderton teachers?

4 Which religious order was founded by Charles Russell?

Answers

1 Priestley.

2 Cain.

3 *Only When I Laugh*.

4 Jesuits.

1 Cavendish.

2 Saul (who became St Paul).

3 *Please Sir!*

4 Jehovah's Witnesses.

LEAGUE QUIZ 8
ROUND 6 – TEAM QUESTIONS

TEAM A

Questions

1 Which type of transport was invented by Gottlieb Daimler?

2 In which country is the Savoy region?

3 In heraldry, which word describes a creature shown on a coat of arms in the sitting position?

4 Which famous actor made his final appearance in a film called *The Naked Edge*?

TEAM B

1 Which type of transport was invented by Igor Sikorsky?

2 In which country is the Lombardy region?

3 In heraldry, which word describes a creature shown on a coat of arms in the lying position?

4 Which famous actor made his final appearance in a film called *Soylent Green*?

Answers

1 The motorcycle.

2 France.

3 Sejant.

4 Gary Cooper.

1 The helicopter.

2 Italy.

3 Couchant.

4 Edward G Robinson.

LEAGUE QUIZ 8

ROUND 7 – INDIVIDUAL QUESTIONS

TEAM A

Questions

1 Name a play by Shakespeare whose title begins and ends with the same vowel.

2 If you belonged to the action group ASH, what would you campaign against?

3 Which bay lies between Canada and Greenland?

4 What is the name of the structure commemorating the 1666 Fire of London?

TEAM B

1 Name a play by Shakespeare whose title begins and ends with the same consonant.

2 If you belonged to the action group CARD, what would you campaign against?

3 Which bay provides the only coastline of Bangladesh?

4 In which thoroughfare did the 1666 Fire of London begin?

Answers

1 *Anthony and Cleopatra* or *Othello.*

2 Smoking.

3 Baffin Bay.

4 The Monument.

1 *The Tempest* or *Twelfth Night.*

2 Racial discrimination.

3 The Bay of Bengal.

4 Pudding Lane.

LEAGUE QUIZ 8
ROUND 8 – TEAM QUESTIONS

TEAM A
Questions
1 Who wrote *Little Women*?

2 Name one of the two acting daughters of Michael Redgrave.

3 Which nautical disaster occurred on 15th April 1912?

4 In which city of the United States is O'Hare International Airport located?

TEAM B

1 Who wrote *Little Dorrit*?

2 Name one of the two acting daughters of John Mills.

3 Which nautical disaster occurred on 6th March 1987?

4 In which city of the United States is Logan International Airport located?

Answers
1 Louisa May Alcott.

2 Vanessa or Lynn.

3 The *Titanic* sank.

4 Chicago.

1 Charles Dickens.

2 Hayley or Juliet.

3 The *Herald of Free Enterprise* sank.

4 Boston.

LEAGUE QUIZ 9
ROUND 1 – TEAM QUESTIONS

TEAM A
Questions

1 Which TV family lived in Stonecave Road in Bedrock?

2 Who had a hit song with *Another Rock & Roll Christmas* in 1984?

3 Which battle occurred in July 1690?

4 What is the French word for twenty?

TEAM B

1 Which TV family lived in Crestview Drive in Beverly Hills?

2 Who had a hit song with *Merry Xmas Everyone* in 1985?

3 Which battle occurred in October 1805?

4 What is the German word for twenty?

Answers

1 The Flintstones.

2 Gary Glitter.

3 The Boyne.

4 Vingt.

1 The Clampetts.

2 Shakin' Stevens.

3 Trafalgar.

4 Zwanzig.

LEAGUE QUIZ 9
ROUND 2 – TEAM QUESTIONS

TEAM A
Questions

1 Which one word is the name of a type of salad and of a famous hotel?

2 Which comedian created the character Basildon Bond?

3 What was the Christian name of gunfighting dentist 'Doc' Holliday?

4 Which new building was built for the 1851 Great Exhibition held in London?

TEAM B

1 Which one word is the name of a brand of biscuit and of a famous hotel?

2 Which comedian created the character Marcel Wave?

3 Give the Christian name of one of Wyatt Earp's two brothers.

4 Which new building was built for the 1925 British Empire Exhibition?

Answers

1 Waldorf.

2 Russ Abbot.

3 John.

4 The Crystal Palace.

1 Ritz.

2 Kenny Everett.

3 Virgil or Morgan.

4 Wembley Stadium.

LEAGUE QUIZ 9
ROUND 3 – INDIVIDUAL QUESTIONS

TEAM A
Questions

1 Solidified carbon dioxide is better known by what other name?

2 In a Jules Verne story, which character went *20,000 Leagues Under the Sea*?

3 On a map, what name is given to lines linking places with an equal amount of sunshine?

4 What is the name of the race of nomadic desert dwellers living in North Africa?

TEAM B

1 Nitrous oxide is better known by what other name?

2 In a Jules Verne story, which character went *Around the World in 80 Days*?

3 On a map, what name is given to lines linking places in the seas that are of equal depth?

4 What is the name of the race of Himalayan mountain dwellers living on the border of Nepal and Tibet?

Answers

1 Dry ice.

2 Captain Nemo.

3 Isohel.

4 Bedouins.

1 Laughing gas.

2 Phineas Fogg.

3 Isobath.

4 Sherpas.

LEAGUE QUIZ 9
ROUND 4 – TEAM QUESTIONS

TEAM A
Questions

1 Astraphobia is a very common fear. Of what?

2 The word epidermis refers to which particular part of the human body?

3 In which film does David Hemmings photograph a murder?

4 In John Constable's famous painting *The Hay Wain*, what is *The Hay Wain*?

TEAM B

1 Acrophobia is a very common fear. Of what?

2 The word plasma refers to which paticular part of the human body?

3 In which film does Oliver Reed take some elephants across the Alps?

4 In Turner's famous painting *The Fighting Temeraire*, what is *The Fighting Temeraire*?

Answers

1 Lightning.

2 The skin.

3 *Blow Up*.

4 A hay cart.

1 Heights.

2 The blood.

3 *Hannibal Brooks*.

4 A warship.

LEAGUE QUIZ 9
ROUND 5 – TEAM QUESTIONS

TEAM A
Questions

1 In which European city can you see the famous Little Mermaid statue?

2 Which singer had a backing group called The Tubeway Army?

3 What name is given to the areas of grassland in South America?

4 The word Helvetia appears on postage stamps from which country?

TEAM B

1 In which European city can you see the Acropolis?

2 Which singer had a backing group called Cockney Rebel?

3 What name is given to the areas of grassland in South Africa?

4 The word Hellas appears on postage stamps from which country?

Answers

1 Copenhagen.

2 Gary Numan.

3 Pampas.

4 Switzerland.

1 Athens.

2 Steve Harley.

3 Veldt.

4 Greece.

LEAGUE QUIZ 9
ROUND 6 – TEAM QUESTIONS

TEAM A
Questions

1 In which year did Channel 4 begin broadcasting in Britain?

2 Which disease is characterised by a deficiency of red blood cells?

3 In the books by James Hilton, what was the full surname of the character known as Mr Chips?

4 How many strings are there on a standard guitar?

TEAM B

1 In which year did breakfast television begin in Britain?

2 Which disease is characterised by an abnormality in the white blood cells?

3 In the books by W E Johns, what was the full surname of the character known as Biggles?

4 How many strings are there on a violin?

Answers

1 1982.

2 Anaemia.

3 Chipping.

4 Six.

1 1983.

2 Leukaemia.

3 Bigglesworth.

4 Four.

LEAGUE QUIZ 9
ROUND 7 – INDIVIDUAL QUESTIONS

TEAM A
Questions

1 For which film did Gary Cooper win his first Oscar as best actor?

2 What type of geographical feature are Hekla, Erebus and Paricutin?

3 Who was the head of the family in the television show *Bonanza*?

4 Who did Winston Churchill describe as 'A half naked fakir'?

TEAM B

1 For which film did Spencer Tracy win his first Oscar as best actor?

2 What type of geographical feature are Minnehaha, Ribbon and Reichenbach?

3 Who was the head of the family in the television show *The High Chaparral*?

4 Who did Winston Churchill describe as 'A sheep in sheep's clothing'?

Answers

1 *Sergeant York.*

2 Volcanoes.

3 Ben Cartwright.

4 Mahatma Gandhi.

1 *Captains Courageous.*

2 Waterfalls.

3 John Cannon.

4 Clement Attlee.

LEAGUE QUIZ 9
ROUND 8 – TEAM QUESTIONS

TEAM A
Questions

1 Which British cathedral has three spires?

2 Which novel by Charles Dickens features the character Smike?

3 What was the capital city of India before New Delhi and Delhi?

4 By what name is Mozart's *Symphony No. 41 in C* better known?

TEAM B

1 Which British cathedral has a clock with no face?

2 Which novel by Charles Dickens features the character Mrs Gamp?

3 What was the capital city of Pakistan before Islamabad?

4 By what name is Beethoven's *Symphony No. 6 in F* better known?

Answers

1 Lichfield.

2 *Nicholas Nickleby*.

3 Calcutta.

4 *Jupiter*.

1 Salisbury.

2 *Martin Chuzzlewit*.

3 Karachi.

4 *Pastoral*.

LEAGUE QUIZ 10
ROUND 1 – TEAM QUESTIONS

TEAM A
Questions

1 Which television show featured a character called Steve Austin?

2 Which bridge spans the harbour of San Francisco?

3 Which band had a number one hit in the 1980s with a song called *China in Your Hand*?

4 What is the medical speciality of a haematologist?

TEAM B

1 Which television show featured a character called Dr David Banner?

2 Which bridge built by I K Brunel spans the Avon?

3 Which band had a number one hit in the 1980s with a song called *Down Under*?

4 What is the medical speciality of a neurologist?

Answers

1 *The Six Million Dollar Man*.

2 The Golden Gate Bridge.

3 T'Pau.

4 The blood.

1 *The Incredible Hulk*.

2 The Clifton Suspension Bridge.

3 Men At Work.

4 The nervous system.

LEAGUE QUIZ 10
ROUND 2 – TEAM QUESTIONS

TEAM A
Questions

1 What is the name given to the fruit which is a cross between a plum and a peach?

2 Who wrote *Lord Jim*?

3 What name is given to a castrated chicken?

4 'Brightly shone the moon that night' is a line from which Christmas carol?

TEAM B

1 What name is given to the fruit which is a cross between a raspberry and a blackberry?

2 Who wrote *Lord of the Flies*?

3 What name is given to a chicken under one year old?

4 'Where a mother laid her baby' is a line from which Christmas carol?

Answers

1 Nectarine.

2 Joseph Conrad.

3 Capon.

4 *Good King Wenceslas.*

1 Loganberry.

2 William Golding.

3 Pullet.

4 *Once in Royal David's City.*

LEAGUE QUIZ 10
ROUND 3 – INDIVIDUAL QUESTIONS

TEAM A
Questions

1 Under what name did Charles Holley have hit records?

2 How often is a census held in Britain?

3 Which famous film first featured the character Rooster Cogburn?

4 How did Charlotte Brew achieve a sporting first?

TEAM B

1 Under what name has Kim Smith had hit records?

2 What name was given to the first census completed in the year 1086?

3 Which famous film was based on the life of John Merrick?

4 How did Sue Brown achieve a sporting first?

Answers

1 Buddy Holly.

2 Every ten years.

3 *True Grit*.

4 She was the first woman to compete in the Grand National.

1 Kim Wilde.

2 The Domesday Book.

3 *The Elephant Man*.

4 She was the first woman to compete in the University Boat Race.

LEAGUE QUIZ 10
ROUND 4 – TEAM QUESTIONS

TEAM A
Questions

1 What was the first name of the German Nazi leader Himmler?

2 What is the present name of what used to be Southern Rhodesia?

3 With which sport do you associate TV commentator Jack Bannister?

4 Who was the female star of the Hitchcock film *Vertigo*?

TEAM B

1 What was the first name of the German Field Marshal Goering?

2 What is the present name of what used to be Northern Rhodesia?

3 With which sport do you associate TV commentator Julian Wilson?

4 Who was the female star of the Hitchcock film *The Birds*?

Answers

1 Heinrich.

2 Zimbabwe.

3 Cricket.

4 Kim Novak.

1 Hermann.

2 Zambia.

3 Horse racing.

4 Tippi Hedren.

LEAGUE QUIZ 10
ROUND 5 – TEAM QUESTIONS

TEAM A
Questions

1 Which company manufactured the famous Spitfire aircraft?

2 Who was the elder brother of James Bond?

3 Which is the largest island belonging to the country of Greece?

4 What do the initials of the famous company ICI stand for?

TEAM B

1 Which company manufactured the famous Hurricane aircraft?

2 Who was the elder brother of Sherlock Holmes?

3 Which is the largest island belonging to the country of Italy?

4 What do the initials of the famous company IBM stand for?

Answers

1 Vickers.

2 Henry.

3 Crete.

4 Imperial Chemical Industries.

1 Hawker.

2 Mycroft.

3 Sicily.

4 International Business Machines.

LEAGUE QUIZ 10
ROUND 6 – TEAM QUESTIONS

TEAM A
Questions

1 After which man is the scale measuring the speed and effects of wind named?

2 Where is the officer training college of the Royal Navy situated?

3 According to an old TV advert, what 'puts the T in Britain'?

4 Which golfer is nicknamed 'The Walrus'?

TEAM B

1 After which man is the scale measuring the strength of earthquakes named?

2 Where is the officer training college of the British Army situated?

3 According to an old TV advert, what 'gives a meal man appeal'?

4 Which golfer is nicknamed 'The Golden Bear'?

Answers

1 Francis Beaufort.

2 Dartmouth.

3 Typhoo tea.

4 Craig Stadler.

1 Charles Richter.

2 Sandhurst.

3 Oxo cubes.

4 Jack Nicklaus.

LEAGUE QUIZ 10
ROUND 7 – INDIVIDUAL QUESTIONS

TEAM A
Questions

1 In the game of charades, how does a player indicate that the word he or she is trying to mime is a person's name?

2 Which river flows along the border between Uruguay and Argentina?

3 What was the name of the American gangster known as 'Pretty Boy'?

4 In which year of the 1960s was the notorious Alcatraz prison closed down?

TEAM B

1 In the game of charades, how does a player indicate that the word he or she is trying to mime sounds like another word?

2 Which river flows along the border between Mexico and the USA?

3 What was the name of the American gangster known as 'Machine Gun'?

4 In which year of the 1960s were the first breathalyser laws introduced?

Answers

1 By tapping the top of his or her head.

2 River Plate.

3 Charles Floyd.

4 1963.

1 By tugging on his or her ear.

2 Rio Grande.

3 George Kelly.

4 1967.

LEAGUE QUIZ 10
ROUND 8 – TEAM QUESTIONS

TEAM A
Questions

1 In which book of the Bible does the death of Moses occur?

2 Which British coin was withdrawn from circulation on 1st January 1970?

3 Who is the patron saint of shoemakers?

4 Which company were the original manufacturers of the Hornet car?

TEAM B

1 In which book of the Bible does the death of Goliath occur?

2 Which British coin was withdrawn from circulation on 30th June 1980?

3 Who is the patron saint of fishermen?

4 Which company were the original manufacturers of the Kestrel car?

Answers

1 Deuteronomy.

2 Half crown.

3 St Crispin.

4 Wolseley.

1 First book of Samuel.

2 Sixpence.

3 St Peter.

4 Riley.

QUICK QUIZZES

	PAGE
General questions	130
Sport questions	160
Pop music questions	170
Themed questions	180

QUICK QUIZ 1

Questions

1 What type of creature is a pipistrelle?
2 Which well known composer wrote only one opera, *Fidelio*?
3 Midsummer Day, Lady Day and Christmas Day are three of the four Quarter Days in England. Which is the fourth?
4 Who did American President Bill Clinton beat in 1996 to secure his second term of office?
5 At which meadow on the bank of the river Thames did King John sign the Magna Carta in 1215?
6 On which island was the government of Fulgencio Batista overthrown in 1959?
7 Who was the first UK winner of the Eurovision Song contest?
8 Which daily newspaper has a drawing of a crusader on the front page?
9 In which city did Oscar Wilde die?
10 Who owned Winnie the Pooh in the A A Milne stories?
11 Which painting style was practised by Renoir and Monet?
12 Which county cricket team play their home fixtures at Grace Road?
13 What was *Genevieve* in the film of the same name?
14 What is regarded as normal body temperature?
15 Name the long-suffering husband of TV's incurable snob Hyacinth Bucket in *Keeping Up Appearances*.
16 In which sport have Nicky Slater and Karen Barber been British champions?
17 How old was Adrian Mole in Sue Townsend's original book?
18 Who won the Ladies' Singles at Wimbledon in 1998 on her third visit to the final?
19 In which year was Mahatma Gandhi murdered?
20 Which word describes a young whale?

Answers

1 It is a bat
2 Beethoven
3 Michaelmas – September 29th
4 Bob Dole
5 Runnymede
6 Cuba – by Fidel Castro
7 Sandie Shaw (*Puppet on a String*)
8 Daily Express
9 Paris
10 Christopher Robin
11 Impressionism
12 Leicestershire
13 A vintage car
14 36.9° Celsius or 98.4° Fahrenheit
15 Richard
16 Ice dancing
17 13¾
18 Jana Novotna
19 1948
20 Calf

QUICK QUIZ 2

Questions

1 Which two archbishops hold the highest offices in the Church of England hierarchy?

2 Which English novelist was originally surnamed Korzeniowski?

3 Who designed the famous Spitfire aircraft?

4 Which is the only monkey living wild in Europe?

5 According to a popular song of 1961, what was 'Wider than a mile'?

6 Which creature represents Scotland on the Royal Arms of Great Britain?

7 Who was the biblical father of Solomon?

8 Which television character portrayed by Jon Pertwee was created by Barbara Euphan Todd?

9 Who composed *Fingal's Cave*?

10 In which mountain range is the country of Andorra situated?

11 In which English city is Temple Meads railway station?

12 John F Kennedy and Jimmy Carter both belonged to the same American political party. Which one?

13 Who won the Oscar for best actor for his part in the 1964 film *My Fair Lady*?

14 Who said in 1974 'I am not a crook'?

15 Who was the supreme god in Roman mythology?

16 Which group of workers was the General Strike of 1926 called in support of?

17 Which is the highest ranking suit in the card game Bridge?

18 Which group had a 1976 number 1 hit with the song *You To Me Are Everything*?

19 Which food product has been advertised on television for a number of years by Tony the tiger?

20 Which car manufacturing company do you associate with the Accord model?

Answers

1 The Archbishop of Canterbury and the Archbishop of York
2 Joseph Conrad
3 R J Mitchell
4 Barbary Ape
5 *Moon River*
6 A unicorn
7 David
8 Worzel Gummidge
9 Felix Mendelssohn
10 Pyrenees
11 Bristol
12 The Democrats
13 Rex Harrison
14 Richard Nixon
15 Jupiter
16 Mineworkers
17 Spades
18 The Real Thing
19 Kellogg's Frosties
20 Honda

QUICK QUIZ 3

Questions

1 Who was the paternal grandfather of Queen Elizabeth II?
2 Who played the television detective Eddie Shoestring?
3 The scarab was sacred to the ancient Egyptians. What kind of creature was it?
4 Which spirit is found in a Tom Collins cocktail?
5 At which American power station was there a serious radiation leak in 1979?
6 Which colour always plays first in chess?
7 Which country officially ceased to exist on Christmas Day 1991?
8 Which group had a 1990 hit with *Listen To Your Heart*?
9 With which sport is Channel 4's *The Morning Line* concerned?
10 Which Irish novelist wrote *The Vicar of Wakefield*?
11 Which English city did the Romans call Deva?
12 Which is the only inanimate star sign?
13 What is the connection between Utopia, Ruritania and Narnia?
14 Who composed *Rhapsody in Blue*?
15 Which river rises at Cross Fell in Cumbria and flows seventy nine miles before entering the North Sea near Middlesbrough?
16 What are rockhoppers and emperors?
17 Which football club is nicknamed 'The Owls'?
18 Where in the body is the patella?
19 Who in history was known as 'The Young Pretender'?
20 Which brewery supplies The Rovers Return in *Coronation Street*?

Answers

1 King George V
2 Trevor Eve
3 A beetle
4 Gin
5 Three Mile Island
6 White
7 USSR
8 Roxette
9 Horse racing
10 Oliver Goldsmith
11 Chester
12 Libra (scales, all the others are animal in form)
13 They are all fictional countries
14 George Gershwin
15 River Tees
16 Species of penguin
17 Sheffield Wednesday
18 Leg (it is the scientific name for the knee cap)
19 Charles Edward Stuart (Bonnie Prince Charlie)
20 Newton and Ridley

QUICK QUIZ 4

Questions

1 What is the alternative name of the German Shepherd dog?

2 In which children's television show could you find characters called George, Zippy and Bungle?

3 Which type of tree is sometimes known as Golden Rain?

4 In which African country is the Serengeti National Park situated?

5 How many heads are there in a standard pack of playing cards?

6 In medieval times the Pilgrims' Way led from Winchester to which other city?

7 In which annual military display do teams from the three armed services compete against each other?

8 Whose real names were Leonard, Arthur, Julius and Herbert?

9 What name is given to a three dimensional image produced by a laser?

10 Who was the Shakespearian sister of Goneril and Regan?

11 Which Englishman is credited with the invention of the military tank?

12 With which sport are Geraldine Rees and Alex Greaves connected?

13 What happens at Buckingham Palace at 11.30 am?

14 Which British general was killed at Khartoum in 1885?

15 The world's highest waterfalls, Angel Falls, are situated in South America. In which country?

16 Who was the evil character in the story of Dr Jekyll and Mr Hyde?

17 What is a yawl?

18 To which composer is the annual Bayreuth festival dedicated?

19 In Roman mythology he was known as Hercules; what what was he known as in Greek mythology?

20 On which motor racing circuit would you encounter Copse, Becketts and Stowe?

Answers
1 Alsatian
2 *Rainbow*
3 Laburnum
4 Tanzania
5 24
6 Canterbury
7 Royal Tournament
8 The Marx brothers
9 A hologram
10 Cordelia
11 Sir Ernest Swinton
12 Horse racing (lady jockeys)
13 The changing of the guard
14 General Charles Gordon
15 Venezuela
16 Mr Hyde
17 A type of yacht
18 Richard Wagner
19 Heracles
20 Silverstone (names of corners)

QUICK QUIZ 5

Questions

1 In Mark Twain's book *The Adventures of Tom Sawyer* what was the name of Tom's girlfriend?

2 What name is given to the signet ring worn by the Pope?

3 In which daily newspaper does *The Gambols* strip cartoon appear?

4 What was the name of the European space probe launched in 1985 to intercept and examine Halley's Comet as it passed in 1986?

5 In which TV show did Rik, Neil and Vyvian share a house?

6 Which competition was held in 1829 to find a locomotive to work on the new Liverpool-Manchester railway line?

7 The largest lake in England can be found in the Lake District. Which is it?

8 Bombadier, goliath and hercules are all types of which insect?

9 Which famous tomb was constructed for the wife of Shah Jehan?

10 According to the Bible who was turned into a pillar of salt for looking back at the cities of Sodom and Gommorah?

11 Who reputedly said 'Let them eat cake'?

12 Which Wimbledon men's champion was nicknamed 'The Iceman'?

13 Which well known criminal was arrested by British police in Rio de Janeiro in 1974?

14 What is a Blenheim orange?

15 What are 'antipodes'?

16 Which is the most common human blood group?

17 In which film did James Cagney say 'Made it ma, top of the world'?

18 Which single word describes an animal or a plant that is a cross between two different varieties or species?

19 One of the most famous men in history died at the age

of thirty five and was buried in an unmarked grave in 1791. Who was he?

20 Who was the third wife of King Henry VIII?

Answers
1 Becky Thatcher
2 The Fisherman's Ring
3 Daily Express
4 Giotto
5 *The Young Ones*
6 The Rainhill Trials (*Rocket* won)
7 Windermere
8 Beetle
9 The Taj Mahal
10 Lot's wife
11 Marie Antoinette (on being told the people had no bread)
12 Bjorn Borg
13 Ronald Biggs
14 A type of apple
15 Places opposite each other on the earth's surface
16 Group O
17 *White Heat*
18 Hybrid
19 Wolfgang Amadeus Mozart
20 Jane Seymour

QUICK QUIZ 6

Questions
1 Who created Baron Frankenstein?
2 How many arms or tentacles has a squid?
3 Who said 'You can't fool all of the people all of the time'?
4 On television, which engine was driven by Casey Jones?
5 In which country were the first World Athletics Championships staged in 1983?
6 Which stretch of water connects the Mediterranean Sea and the Atlantic Ocean?
7 Which American group have had hits with *Africa* and *Hold the Line*?
8 Where in London does the annual Trooping the Colour ceremony take place?
9 What name is given to the art form which involves painting inanimate objects?
10 At some time almost everybody will have used a machine known as an ATM. What is it?
11 What are sometimes referred to as 'The backbone of England'?
12 Who was the biblical mother of King Solomon?
13 Who has played television characters called Robin Tripp and Simon Harrap?
14 Which is the smallest member of the monkey family?
15 Of what are Desiree and Pentland Crown varieties?
16 Which disease killed Prince Albert, Franz Schubert and Arnold Bennett?
17 Which Belgian detective was created by Agatha Christie?
18 Which European city is known as 'The Eternal City'?
19 'Impatiens' is the scientific name of a popular household plant, what is its everyday name?
20 Which drink is composed of vodka and tomato juice?

Answers

1 Mary Shelley
2 Ten
3 Abraham Lincoln
4 *Cannonball Express*
5 Finland
6 Straits of Gibraltar
7 Toto
8 Horse Guards Parade
9 Still life
10 A bank cash dispensing machine
   (Automated telling machine)
11 The Pennines
12 Bathsheba
13 Richard O'Sullivan
14 The (pygmy) marmoset
15 Potatoes
16 Typhoid
17 Hercule Poirot
18 Rome
19 Busy lizzie
20 Bloody Mary

QUICK QUIZ 7

Questions
1 Who created the detective Lord Peter Wimsey?
2 Found in the human body, what type of substances are adrenaline and oestrogen?
3 Which well known comedian committed suicide in a Sydney hotel room in 1968?
4 Which bird has varieties called mallard, widgeon and shoveler?
5 What is the name of the sacred Sikh building in Amritsar?
6 What was the invention of English mathematician William Oughtred?
7 Which is the lowest voice in male singing?
8 Of which TV family were John and Olivia the parents?
9 Which is the closest planet to earth?
10 Who played the king in the film *The King and I*?
11 On which river does the city of Cambridge stand?
12 In which city did the notorious grave robbers Burke and Hare ply their trade?
13 Who wrote the 'Reggie Perrin' series of books?
14 What were the first names of the Everly Brothers?
15 What is separated from the English mainland by the Solent?
16 Which four times Wimbledon champion was nick-named 'The Rocket'?
17 Which of the four gospel authors was a tax collector?
18 According to a well known song, how long is Camp-town racetrack?
19 If you were convicted of larceny what would you have done?
20 What type of transport is a VLCC?

Answers

1 Dorothy L Sayers
2 Hormones
3 Tony Hancock
4 The duck
5 The Golden Temple
6 The slide rule
7 Bass
8 The Walton family in *The Waltons*
9 Venus
10 Yul Brynner
11 Cam
12 Edinburgh
13 David Nobbs
14 Phil and Don
15 Isle of Wight
16 Rod Laver
17 Matthew
18 Five miles long
19 Stolen something
20 An oil transporting ship (Very Large Crude Carrier)

QUICK QUIZ 8

Questions

1 Which of the Brontë sisters wrote *Agnes Grey*?
2 Which television character had children named Billy, Joey, Jack, Adrian and Aveline?
3 Which weepie film contains the dialogue 'Love means never having to say you're sorry'?
4 In which country could you visit the Alhambra?
5 Which gas do plants absorb from the atmosphere?
6 To which family of instruments does the saxophone belong?
7 Where did Hitler, Chamberlain, Daladier and Mussolini meet in 1938?
8 In which year of the 1980s were CB radios legalised in Britain?
9 Which group had a 1985 top ten hit with *Something About You*?
10 Wyoming, West Virginia, Washington: which other American state begins with the letter 'W'?
11 If you travelled directly west from London, which would be the first country you would reach?
12 In T S Eliot's play *Murder in the Cathedral*, who was murdered?
13 Who played private eye Matt Helm in *The Silencers*?
14 Which organisation has the motto 'Fidelity Bravery Integrity'?
15 After which German count was a type of large motor driven airship named?
16 By what name is the Gravelly Hill interchange more usually known?
17 What name is given to the young of a goose?
18 Which is the highest mountain in the continent of Africa?
19 What is the alternative name of ascorbic acid?
20 Which was the first country other than the West Indies to win the world cup for cricket?

Answers

1 Anne Brontë
2 Nellie Boswell (in *Bread*)
3 *Love Story*
4 Spain
5 Carbon dioxide
6 Woodwind
7 Munich
8 1981
9 Level 42
10 Wisconsin
11 Canada
12 Thomas A'Becket (in Canterbury)
13 Dean Martin
14 FBI (Federal Bureau of Investigation)
15 Ferdinand Zeppelin
16 Spaghetti Junction
17 Gosling
18 Mount Kilimanjaro
19 Vitamin C
20 India (in 1983)

QUICK QUIZ 9

Questions
1 Which female singer had a 1978 hit with *Lilac Wine*?
2 Which game begins with a tip off?
3 To which family of birds does the robin belong?
4 What are clove hitch, sheet bend and running bowline varieties of?
5 During World War II what was the Luftwaffe?
6 Which legendary island was said to have been situated to the west of the Pillars of Hercules?
7 From what are pomphret cakes made?
8 What can be simple, compound, impacted or greenstick?
9 Which Shakespeare play features the female character Portia?
10 Which English King was responsible for making the sovereign the head of the Church of England?
11 In which event did Steve Ovett win an Olympic gold medal for Britain?
12 What is the more common name of the Charles Dickens character John Dawkins?
13 On television what was the name of Frank Spencer's baby daughter?
14 Which position is held by the Primate of England?
15 What was the sequel to the film *Funny Girl*?
16 In which country would you find the major part of the Atacama desert?
17 Which national organisation has the motto 'Courtesy and care'?
18 Which metal is an alloy of copper and tin?
19 Which month of the year is named after a Roman goddess?
20 In Britain they are known as crisps; what are they called in America?

Answers

1 Elkie Brooks
2 Basketball
3 Thrush
4 Knots
5 German Airforce
6 Atlantis
7 Liquorice
8 Fractures of a bone
9 *The Merchant of Venice*
10 Henry VIII
11 800 metres (Moscow 1980)
12 The Artful Dodger
13 Jessica
14 Archbishop of York
15 *Funny Lady*
16 Chile
17 Automobile Association
18 Bronze
19 June (after Juno)
20 Potato chips

QUICK QUIZ 10

Questions

1 Who was the first Englishman to become Embassy world professional darts champion?

2 Which famous horse was created by Anna Sewell?

3 In which country is the skiing resort of St Moritz?

4 Who did Ronald Reagan defeat in the 1984 American presidential election to win his second term of office?

5 In which Disney cartoon film can you hear the song *Give A Little Whistle*?

6 What name is commonly given to the area around Stoke on Trent?

7 What was the nickname of American gangster George Kelly?

8 Which group had a 1985 hit with *Don't Look Down*?

9 In which daily newspaper can you see the cartoon strip *Beau Peep*?

10 Which group had a 1980 hit with *Special Brew*?

11 Which branch of chemistry deals with carbon compounds?

12 What was the nickname of American gangster John Diamond?

13 Who had the following three husbands: Francis II of France, Lord Darnley and the Earl of Boswell?

14 In which film did Clint Eastwood say 'Go ahead punk, make my day'?

15 In mythology, whose touch could turn things to gold?

16 What is a Green Goddess?

17 Which word describes a long narrow inlet of sea surrounded by steep cliffs?

18 What connects the names Ramsay, Fisher, Coggan and Temple?

19 What is the name of the lighthouse located four miles south west of the Scilly Isles?

20 In the human body, what are capillaries?

Answers

 1 John Lowe
 2 Black Beauty
 3 Switzerland
 4 Walter Mondale
 5 *Pinocchio*
 6 The Potteries
 7 'Machine Gun'
 8 Go West
 9 Daily Star
10 Bad Manners
11 Organic chemistry
12 'Legs'
13 Mary, Queen of Scots (Mary Stuart)
14 *Dirty Harry*
15 King Midas'
16 An army fire engine
17 Fjord
18 They have all been Archbishop of Canterbury
19 Bishop's Rock
20 Minute blood vessels

QUICK QUIZ 11

Questions
1 Which notorious prison stood on a rock in San Francisco Bay?
2 On which island did the Bay of Pigs invasion take place in 1961?
3 Which English King compiled the Domesday Book?
4 Which male soap opera character had four children named Adam, Stephen, Fallon and Amanda?
5 Who had a 1973 hit with the song *Get Down*?
6 Who succeeded Joe Gormley in 1981 as president of the NUM?
7 According to Greek mythology, how many rivers were there in Hades?
8 In *Treasure Island* who finds the treasure?
9 In which year did Elvis Presley marry Priscilla Beaulieu?
10 Who played the title role in *The Glenn Miller Story*?
11 Which sculptor's works include *The Thinker* and *The Kiss*?
12 Which number cavalry were massacred at the Little Big Horn?
13 Which ancient Greek physician is regarded as the father of medicine?
14 The daughter of playwright Eugene O'Neill married a tramp. Why was he not unduly upset?
15 In which year was the American embassy in Teheran occupied by Iranian students?
16 In which city is La Scala opera house?
17 What is the explosive result of mixing charcoal, saltpetre and sulphur?
18 What is a hydrometer used to measure?
19 Into which sea does the river Danube flow?
20 From which country did America purchase the territory of Louisiana?

Answers

1 Alcatraz
2 Cuba
3 William I (the Conqueror)
4 Blake Carrington (in *Dynasty*)
5 Gilbert O'Sullivan
6 Arthur Scargill
7 Five
8 Ben Gunn
9 1967 (May 1st)
10 James Stewart
11 Auguste Rodin's
12 7th
13 Hippocrates
14 The tramp in question was Charlie Chaplin
15 1979
16 Milan
17 Gunpowder
18 Specific gravity of liquids
19 Black Sea
20 France

QUICK QUIZ 12

Questions

1 If a cockney offered you some 'Rosie', what would you expect to receive?
2 In which film did Humphrey Bogart say 'Here's looking at you kid'?
3 In which famous book is one of the major characters called Winston Smith?
4 What, in a geographical sense, are the Negev and the Nubian?
5 Who do you associate with the phrase 'Time and relative dimensions in space'?
6 In which year was the world's first heart transplant carried out?
7 Which group had a 1966 hit with *God Only Knows*?
8 For what particular ability is the secretary bird well known?
9 Which English King purchased Buckingham Palace for the monarchy?
10 Whose world chess title did Gary Kasparov take in 1985?
11 What is a yellowhammer?
12 Who was the legendary Roman slave who was reputed to have removed a thorn from the paw of a lion?
13 What is the name of the principal geological fault running through the American state of California?
14 What name is given to the Pope's personal body-guard?
15 Which successful group is composed of three brothers called Barry, Maurice and Robin?
16 What do vertebrate animals possess that invertebrate animals do not?
17 What is the collective name given to the chemical elements radon, xenon, krypton, helium, argon and neon?
18 In a speech on May 13th 1940 Winston Churchill said 'I have nothing to offer but blood, toil, tears and . . .' what?

19 What do the following have in common: Sole, Port-
land, Dover, Tyne?
20 Which museum is situated at Beaulieu?

Answers
1 Tea (Rosie Lee)
2 *Casablanca*
3 *1984*
4 Deserts
5 Dr Who (The initials spell TARDIS, the name of his craft)
6 1967
7 The Beach Boys
8 It is known for its ability to kill snakes
9 George III
10 Anatoly Karpov's
11 A bird
12 Androcles
13 San Andreas fault
14 Swiss Guard
15 Bee Gees
16 A backbone
17 Inert gases
18 Sweat
19 They are shipping forecast areas around the British coast
20 National Motor Museum

QUICK QUIZ 13

Questions

1 Which French king was executed during the French Revolution?

2 To which group of islands do Majorca and Minorca belong?

3 Who created the cartoon cat Garfield?

4 According to the well known rhyme who are made of 'frogs and snails and puppy dogs' tails'?

5 With which medical breakthrough is the name of Edward Jenner associated?

6 Where does Postman Pat deliver letters?

7 Who had a 1979 hit with the song *Oliver's Army*?

8 In which county is the royal residence of Sandringham?

9 A joey is the name given to the young of which animal?

10 Which peak overlooks the city of Cape Town?

11 Who wrote *The History of Mr Polly*?

12 What breed of dog took the title role in the 1992 film *Beethoven*?

13 What is the purpose of a Roman Catholic conclave?

14 In what year did the ½p decimal coin cease to be legal currency in the UK?

15 How many overs are each side allowed in Sunday League cricket?

16 Who played a teacher called Bernard Hedges on television?

17 Which gas makes up the largest part of the air we breathe?

18 Which film studio made the Bugs Bunny cartoons?

19 A numismatist is a collector of what?

20 Which city is connected to London by the M3 motorway?

Answers

1 Louis XVI
2 Balearic islands
3 Jim Davis
4 Little boys
5 Vaccination
6 Greendale
7 Elvis Costello
8 Norfolk
9 Kangaroo
10 Table Mountain
11 H G Wells
12 St Bernard
13 To elect a new Pope
14 1984
15 Forty
16 John Alderton
17 Nitrogen
18 Warner Brothers
19 Coins
20 Southampton

QUICK QUIZ 14

Questions
1 For what is the name of George Hepplewhite remembered?
2 In which athletic event has Bob Seagren been Olympic champion?
3 In what year did the Channel Tunnel open for business?
4 In which park did Yogi Bear and Boo-Boo live?
5 Which British king reigned for sixty years?
6 Which is the first of the ten commandments?
7 On which Mediterranean island was Gerald Durrell's book *My Family and Other Animals* set?
8 Which is the world's second most spoken language after Chinese?
9 Who designed ships called *Great Britain* and *Great Western*?
10 Which school did Billy Bunter attend in the stories by Frank Richards?
11 In which range of hills is the famous Cheddar Gorge?
12 Which group had a 1981 hit with *Vienna*?
13 In which city would you watch a football match between teams nicknamed The Pirates and The Robins?
14 Which King of England did Guy Fawkes attempt to blow up?
15 What was the painter Rembrandt's first name?
16 Who played the title role in the 1995 film *Ace Ventura Pet Detective*?
17 What can be measured on an instrument called a pluviometer?
18 Who is credited with the invention of the miner's safety lamp?
19 What type of creature was Henry Williamson's Tarka?
20 After which man was Rhodesia named?

Answers

1 Furniture (he was a cabinet maker)
2 Pole Vault
3 1994
4 Jellystone National Park
5 George III
6 'Thou shalt have no other god but me'
7 Corfu
8 English
9 I K Brunel
10 Greyfriars
11 The Mendips
12 Ultravox
13 Bristol (Bristol Rovers – Pirates, Bristol City – Robins)
14 James I
15 Rembrandt! (He was called Rembrandt Van Rijn)
16 Jim Carrey
17 Rainfall
18 Sir Humphrey Davy
19 An otter (in *Tarka the Otter*)
20 Cecil Rhodes

QUICK QUIZ 15

Questions
1 Which football club plays at the Riverside Stadium?
2 Which popular children's characters were created by Roger Hargreaves?
3 What name was given to the treaty signed by eight Eastern bloc countries in 1955?
4 Who shot and killed Jesse James?
5 Which group of Portuguese islands includes Porto Santo?
6 Which group had a 1982 hit with *Mad World*?
7 What was the sequel to the film *Spartacus*?
8 What takes place in the Bavarian village of Oberammergau every ten years?
9 Who wrote the story *The Ugly Duckling*?
10 In which war did the Battle of Edgehill take place?
11 What in the Bible was made out of gopher wood?
12 Who invented all of James Bond's special gadgets?
13 Identify this creature: the male is called a cob, the female a pen and the young a cygnet.
14 What name is given to the fruit of the beech tree?
15 In which county is the highest point in England?
16 What are the names of the two bones located between the knee and the ankle?
17 Which fruit-producing plant grows leaves around ten feet long?
18 What was the surname of the composer brothers Edward, Joseph and Johann?
19 Which high street store uses the St Michael trademark?
20 Name one of the two chemical elements that are in a liquid state at room temperature.

Answers

1 Middlesbrough
2 Mister Men
3 Warsaw Pact
4 Bob Ford
5 Madeira Islands
6 Tears For Fears
7 *Son of Spartacus*
8 The Passion Play
9 Hans Christian Anderson
10 English Civil War
11 Noah's Ark
12 Q
13 Swan
14 Mast
15 Cumbria (Scafell Pike)
16 Fibula and tibia
17 Banana
18 Strauss
19 Marks & Spencer
20 Mercury or bromine

QUICK QUIZ – SPORT 1

Questions

1 Which England football striker was nicknamed 'Sniffer'?
2 Which British athlete won two silver medals during the 1996 Atlanta Olympic Games?
3 Who scored 309 runs on the first day of a test match at Headingley in 1930?
4 Against which American boxer did Frank Bruno suffer the first defeat of his professional career?
5 Which historic sporting event occurred at Iffley Road, Oxford in 1954?
6 The 1951 film *Follow the Sun* was a fictionalised biography of which famous golfer?
7 Which English tennis player defeated Bjorn Borg at Wimbledon?
8 Which is always the last of the five English horse racing classics to be contested each season?
9 In which event did Sean Kerly win Olympic gold in 1988?
10 Which sport is divided into periods of play known as chukkas?
11 In which city is the famous Bislett athletics stadium situated?
12 Chemics v Wires: a possible match in which sport?
13 Who made the first maximum break recorded during the Embassy World Professional Snooker Championships?
14 Which British driver first won the Formula 1 Drivers' Championship for Colin Chapman's Lotus team?
15 What was the specialist stroke of British Olympic swimming champion Duncan Goodhew?
16 Who missed a penalty during the 1988 FA Cup final?
17 Which horse did Frankie Dettori ride to victory in both the English Derby and the Prix de l'Arc de Triomphe in 1995?
18 Where would you encounter 'The Valley of Sin'?
19 Which sport begins with a 'Face off'?

20 Lester Piggott rode his last Derby winner in 1983; what was it called?

Answers
 1 Allan Clarke
 2 Roger Black
 3 Don Bradman
 4 James 'Bonecrusher' Smith
 5 The four minute barrier for the mile was broken for the first time by Roger Bannister
 6 Ben Hogan
 7 Roger Taylor
 8 St Leger
 9 Hockey (as a member of Great Britain's successful men's team)
10 Polo
11 Oslo, Norway
12 Rugby League
13 Cliff Thorburn
14 Jim Clark in 1963
15 Breaststroke
16 John Aldridge of Liverpool
17 Lammtarra
18 On the 18th hole at St Andrew's golf club
19 Ice hockey
20 Teenoso

QUICK QUIZ – SPORT 2

Questions

1 Steven Redgrave won the Olympic gold medal for coxless pairs rowing at the Olympic Games of 1988, 1992 and 1996. Who was his partner on the occasion of his first victory?

2 Who did Frank Bruno defeat to finally realise his dream of becoming world heavyweight champion?

3 In which sport has England's Gary Havelock been a world champion?

4 Which well known comedian owned the 1994 Grand National winning horse Miinnehoma?

5 Who scored the goal in the 1996 FA Cup final that earned Manchester United the league and cup double?

6 Who was beaten by a record score of 18 frames to 3 in the World Snooker Championship final of 1989?

7 Which English football club is nicknamed 'The Quakers'?

8 Whose record score for a single test match innings did Brian Lara break when he scored 375 against England at Antigua?

9 Who is the 'Great White Shark' of professional golf?

10 Where is the US Open Tennis Championship staged?

11 Who won a shooting gold medal for Britain at the Olympic Games of 1984 and 1988?

12 Which country stages Grand Prix motor racing at the Kyalami circuit?

13 Which cyclist won the Tour de France in five consecutive years between 1991 and 1995?

14 Which is always the last event of an athletics decathlon?

15 Which country is represented by the Pumas Rugby Union team?

16 Which football club were the first ever English Premier League champions?

17 What is the minimum number of points required to win a tie break in tennis?

18 Who inflicted the first professional defeat on Muhammad Ali?

19 In which yachting class were Mike McIntyre and Bryn Vaile Olympic champions in 1988?

20 Who was the first batsman to amass 10,000 runs in test cricket?

Answers

1 Andrew Holmes (Matthew Pinsent on the other two occasions)
2 Oliver McCall
3 Speedway in 1992
4 Freddie Starr
5 Eric Cantona
6 John Parrott (by Steve Davis)
7 Darlington
8 Sir Gary Sobers' (365 not out)
9 Greg Norman
10 Flushing Meadow
11 Malcolm Cooper (small bore rifle, three position)
12 South Africa
13 Miguel Indurain
14 1,500 metres
15 Argentina
16 Manchester United
17 7
18 Joe Frazier
19 Star class
20 Sunil Gavaskar

QUICK QUIZ – SPORT 3

Questions

1 How many players are there on each side in the Ryder Cup?

2 Which England striker scored five times in a match against Cyprus in 1975?

3 Which top jockey had his only success when steering Shirley Heights to Epsom glory in 1978?

4 Which British 100 metres Olympic champion was one of the subjects of the film *Chariots of Fire*?

5 Who was the first Brazilian driver to become Formula 1 world champion?

6 Regarded by many as the finest player never to have won Wimbledon, he was defeated in the final on four occasions. His last defeat was in 1974 at the hands of Jimmy Connors. Name him.

7 Which English county did New Zealand cricketer Sir Richard Hadlee represent?

8 Which man won a record seven gold medals in the swimming events at the Munich Olympic Games of 1972?

9 What was the real first name of baseball star Babe Ruth?

10 In which weight division did Chris Finnegan win a boxing gold medal at Mexico City in 1968?

11 Dracula v The Grinder: which sport?

12 In which city do Italian football club Juventus play their home matches?

13 What was the cricketing speciality of Indian test player Farokh Engineer?

14 On which Scottish golf course could you play the famous 'Postage stamp' hole?

15 Who was the first female gymnast to receive a perfect score of 10 for her beam routine during the Montreal Olympics?

16 Which British boxer lost his world title to Steve Cruz?

17 What is the lowest number of darts required to complete a game of 501?

18 What nationality is former skiing champion Franz Klammer?
19 Who does horse racing pundit John McCrirrick refer to as 'Great One'?
20 Who won the men's 110m hurdles event at the first three World Athletics Championships?

Answers
1 12
2 Malcolm Macdonald
3 Greville Starkey
4 Harold Abrahams
5 Emerson Fittipaldi
6 Ken Rosewall
7 Nottinghamshire
8 Mark Spitz
9 Herman
10 Middleweight
11 Snooker (Ray Reardon v Cliff Thorburn)
12 Turin
13 Wicketkeeping
14 Troon
15 Nadia Comaneci
16 Barry McGuigan
17 9
18 Austrian
19 John Francome
20 Greg Foster

QUICK QUIZ – SPORT 4

Questions

1 Who introduced a new style of highjumping that revolutionised the sport in the late 1960s?

2 In 1994, who became the first South African winner of the US Open Golf Championship since Gary Player in 1965?

3 Which Scottish football club did Alex Ferguson leave to join Manchester United?

4 On which racecourse is the Prix de l'Arc de Triomphe run?

5 In the 1988 Olympics, who won two gold medals for diving, despite hitting his head on the platform during one of his dives?

6 Which country were the first ever winners of the World Cup for Rugby Union in 1987?

7 Which England batsman was nicknamed 'Arkle'?

8 In which year were Wimbledon football club elected to the English League?

9 In which sport has Mike Hazelwood of England been a world champion?

10 Why is the 1969 match between Pancho Gonzales and Charlie Pasarell remarkable in Wimbledon tennis history?

11 Which British world lightweight champion lost his title to Alexis Arguello of Nicaragua in 1981?

12 Which number is opposite 11 on a dartboard?

13 Which motor racing circuit is nicknamed 'The Brick-yard'?

14 Which trophy is contested annually between the Rugby Union teams of England and Scotland?

15 Which is the oldest racecourse in England?

16 Who in the 1960s and 70s formed a very successful tennis doubles partnership with Tony Roche?

17 On which make of bike did Barry Sheene become world 500cc motor cycling champion in 1976/7?

18 In which sport was Jill Hammersley an England international?

19 With impeccable timing, Geoff Boycott scored the 100th century of his career in front of his home crowd at Headingley in 1977. Who were the opposition on that day?

20 Who did Stephen Hendry defeat to win his fifth world snooker title in 1995?

Answers

1 Dick Fosbury (Fosbury flop)
2 Ernie Els
3 Aberdeen
4 Longchamps
5 Greg Louganis
6 New Zealand
7 Derek Randall
8 1977
9 Water skiing
10 It was the longest ever match, lasting 5 hours and 12 minutes. This was before the advent of the modern day tie break rule.
11 Jim Watt
12 6
13 Indianapolis
14 Calcutta Cup
15 Chester
16 John Newcombe
17 Suzuki
18 Table tennis
19 Australia
20 Nigel Bond

QUICK QUIZ – SPORT 5

Questions

1 Which country won the inaugural World Cup for cricket?

2 By what name is the 6th fence in the Grand National known?

3 How many points are awarded for a cannon in billiards?

4 What is the name of the Maori war dance performed by the All Blacks rugby union team immediately prior to their matches?

5 In baseball, what is contested annually by the winners of the American and National Leagues?

6 Which former world darts champion is nicknamed 'The Limestone Cowboy'?

7 Who scored a goal from inside his own half on the opening day of the 1996-1997 FA Carling Premiership season?

8 In 1968, Glamorgan bowler Malcolm Nash approached the wicket to bowl the first ball of an over to Gary Sobers. What happened next?

9 In which sport could you witness a triple axel?

10 Who was known as 'The Hit Man From Detroit'?

11 Which sport is the subject of the film *This Sporting Life*?

12 England won the 1966 Football World Cup by defeating West Germany 4–2 in the final, but who did they beat in the semi-final?

13 Who was the first British Formula 1 world drivers' champion?

14 Which British female athlete won silver and bronze medals during the 1995 World Athletics Championships?

15 Which female swimmer won the 100m freestyle gold medal at three consecutive Olympic Games, 1956, 1960 and 1964?

16 In which of the one day cricket competitions are each team allowed to bowl sixty overs?

17 What horse did Red Rum overtake on the run-in on the occasion of his first Grand National victory in 1973?
18 What happened to the Italian runner Pietro Dorando after he won the marathon at the London Olympics of 1908?
19 In which sport was American Hank Aaron a legend?
20 Who did Arthur Ashe beat in the final to become Wimbledon champion in 1975?

Answers
 1 West Indies in 1975
 2 Becher's Brook
 3 2
 4 The Haka
 5 World Series
 6 Bob Anderson
 7 David Beckham (Wimbledon v Manchester Utd)
 8 Sobers hit every ball of the over for 6. The first time this feat had been achieved.
 9 Ice skating
10 Boxer Thomas Hearns
11 Rugby League
12 Portugal (2–1, both goals from Bobby Charlton)
13 Mike Hawthorn in 1958
14 Kelly Holmes
15 Dawn Fraser of Australia
16 Nat West Bank Trophy
17 Crisp
18 He was disqualified after being helped across the finishing line by officials
19 Baseball
20 Jimmy Connors

QUICK QUIZ – POP MUSIC 1

Questions

1 Marvin Aday has had a number of hits in the British charts. By what name is he better known?
2 Which successful group were often referred to by the letters OMD?
3 Which was the first British chart entry for Madonna?
4 Which English singer appeared live during BOTH the British and American Live Aid concerts of 1985?
5 What is the connection between the following songs: *Je T'aime, Relax, My Ding-a-Ling*?
6 Who performed their Farewell Concert at Wembley on June 28th 1986?
7 What is the real name of Bono of U2?
8 What was the name of Johnny Kidd's backing group?
9 Which Beatles album cover has a photograph of them walking on a zebra crossing?
10 Who sang lead vocals on the Python Lee Jackson hit *In A Broken Dream*?
11 On July 3rd 1982 a song from the musical *South Pacific* jumped from number 33 to number 1 in the charts. Who sang it?
12 Which band had a top ten hit in 1986 with a cover of the Led Zeppelin classic *Stairway To Heaven*?
13 Whose vital statistics were 42-39-56?
14 From which Queen album was their biggest hit *Bohemian Rhapsody* taken?
15 Johnny Wakelin had a hit with the song *Black Superman*. To which sportsman was it a tribute?
16 For which band did Helen O'Hara play the violin?
17 Gordon Sumner, Andy Summers and Stewart Copeland formed which successful group?
18 Which group's first top ten hit was *Stay* in 1963?
19 The Rolling Stones recorded a song called *2120 South Michigan Avenue* as a tribute to which recording company?

20 Which song first entered the British charts in November of 1957, and eventually reached number 1 in November of 1986?

Answers
1 Meatloaf
2 Orchestral Manoeuvres in the Dark
3 *Holiday*
4 Phil Collins
5 They were all banned
6 Wham!
7 Paul Hewson
8 The Pirates
9 *Abbey Road*
10 Rod Stewart
11 Captain Sensible (*Happy Talk*)
12 Far Corporation
13 Rosie (in the AC/DC song *Whole Lotta Rosie*)
14 *A Night At The Opera*
15 Muhammad Ali
16 Dexy's Midnight Runners
17 Police
18 The Hollies
19 Chess (it was the address of the studio)
20 *Reet Petite* by Jackie Wilson

QUICK QUIZ – POP MUSIC 2 – LYRICS

Identify the number 1 hits from the lyric extracts.

Questions

1 'Lips that promise fear the worst, tongue so sharp the bubble burst . . .' – 1990
2 'When I was just a little girl I asked my mother what will I be . . .' – 1956
3 'There's a moose loose aboot this hoose . . .' – 1958
4 'I want you to know that since you walked out on me I'm so lonesome every day . . .' – 1961
5 'You dream maker you old heartbreaker wherever you're going I'm going your way . . .' – 1961
6 'Please lock me away and don't allow the day here inside where I hide . . .' – 1964
7 'One fine day I'm gonna be the one to make you understand I'm gonna be your man . . .' – 1966
8 'Then I awake and look around me all the four grey walls that surround me . . .' – 1966
9 'If you look out your window tonight pull on the string with the note that's attached to my heart . . .' – 1971
10 'Nothing means more to me than hearing you say I want to marry you, will you marry me uncle Ray . . .' – 1972
11 'We've been together since we were nine or ten together we climbed hills and trees . . .' – 1974
12 'Don't you tell it to the trees or they will tell the birds and bees and everyone will know . . .' – 1975
13 'Far have I travelled and much have I seen dark distant mountains and valleys of green . . .' – 1977
14 'In the silence of your room, in the darkness of your schemes, you must only think of me . . .' – 1992
15 'In my life there's been heartache and pain I don't know if I can face it again . . .' – 1986
16 'I guess there is no one to blame we're leaving ground will things ever be the same again . . .' – 1986
17 'I picked up the phone and dialled your number, not sure to put it down or speak . . .' – 1993

18 'Darling I promise you this I'll send you all my love every day in a letter . . .' – 1989
19 'Something has invaded my life, cutting its way through my dreams like a knife . . .' – 1989
20 'There won't be snow in Africa this Christmas time . . .' – 1989

Answers

1 *A Little Time* by The Beautiful South
2 *Whatever Will Be Will Be* by Doris Day
3 *Hoots Mon* by Lord Rockingham's XI
4 *Walk Right Back* by The Everley Brothers
5 *Moon River* by Danny Williams
6 *World Without Love* by Peter and Gordon
7 *Keep On Running* by Spencer Davis Group
8 *Green Green Grass Of Home* by Tom Jones
9 *Knock Three Times* by Dawn
10 *Clair* by Gilbert O'Sullivan
11 *Seasons In The Sun* by Terry Jacks
12 *Whispering Grass* by Windsor Davies and Don Estelle
13 *Mull Of Kintyre* by Wings
14 *Stay* by Shakespeare's Sister
15 *I Want To Know What Love Is* by Foreigner
16 *The Final Countdown* by Europe
17 *Babe* by Take That
18 *Sealed With A Kiss* Jason Donovan
19 *Something's Gotten Hold Of My Heart* by Marc Almond with Gene Pitney
20 *Do They Know It's Christmas?* by Band Aid

QUICK QUIZ – POP MUSIC 3 –
NAME ORIGINS

Which successful groups took their names from the following?

Questions
1 A character from the Dickens novel *David Copper-field*?
2 The initial letters of the first names of the four band members?
3 Two characters from *Herge's Adventures of Tin Tin*?
4 The unemployment benefit form?
5 The title of a novel by Herman Hesse?
6 The title of a John Wayne film?
7 A type of American fire engine?
8 A popular type of motor scooter?
9 An underworld river in Greek mythology?
10 A character from the television series *Star Trek*?
11 An island off the coast of Northumberland?
12 The title of a French fashion magazine?
13 A western film directed by Robert Benton?
14 A torture device used in medieval times?
15 The slang term used by musicians for saxophonists?
16 The inventor of the agricultural drill?
17 An Australian television detective?
18 The financial situation of the band early in their career?
19 The children of casual oil well workers in Oklahoma?
20 A type of cocktail made from orange juice and champagne?

Answers

 1 Uriah Heep
 2 Abba
 3 Thompson Twins
 4 UB40
 5 Steppenwolf
 6 The Searchers
 7 REO Speedwagon
 8 Lambrettas
 9 Styx
10 T'Pau
11 Lindisfarne
12 Depeche Mode
13 Bad Company
14 Iron Maiden
15 Blow Monkeys
16 Jethro Tull
17 Boney M
18 Dire Straits
19 Boomtown Rats
20 Bucks Fizz

QUICK QUIZ – POP MUSIC 4 –
REAL NAMES

The real names of twenty successful musicians are given below. By what names are (or were) they better known?

Questions
1 Harry Webb
2 William Broad
3 Marie Lawrie
4 David Cook
5 Frederick Bulsara
6 Robert Zimmerman
7 John Lydon
8 Richard Starkey
9 Yorgos Kyriakou Panayioutu
10 Terence Nelhams
11 Michael Barrett
12 Stuart Goddard
13 Gerry Dorsey
14 Vincent Furnier
15 Elaine Bookbinder
16 Sandra Goodrich
17 Annie May Bullock
18 Raymond Burns
19 Reginald Dwight
20 Declan McManus

Answers

1 Cliff Richard
2 Billy Idol
3 Lulu
4 David Essex
5 Freddy Mercury
6 Bob Dylan
7 Johnny Rotten
8 Ringo Starr
9 George Michael
10 Adam Faith
11 Shakin' Stevens
12 Adam Ant
13 Engelbert Humperdinck
14 Alice Cooper
15 Elkie Brooks
16 Sandie Shaw
17 Tina Turner
18 Captain Sensible
19 Elton John
20 Elvis Costello

QUICK QUIZ – POP MUSIC 5 –
SAME TITLES

The following pairs of artistes have both had a chart hit with a song with the same title, though they are two different songs. Give the title in each case.

Questions
1 The Jam 1981, David Bowie 1986
2 Earth, Wind and Fire 1979, Princess 1985
3 The Beatles 1964, Wet Wet Wet 1990
4 Dickie Valentine 1955, Brenda Lee 1963
5 Elvis Presley 1961, Diana Ross 1971
6 Roxy Music 1973, The Crusaders 1979
7 Elvis Presley 1960, Lionel Richie 1984
8 The Platters 1956, Yazoo 1982
9 The Temptations 1965, Madness 1980
10 The Everly Brothers 1961, Heaven 17 1983
11 Frankie Avalon 1959, Bananarama 1986
12 Howard Jones 1983, Dee-Lite 1990
13 Mud 1973, Seal 1990
14 Blondie 1980, Spagna 1987
15 The Commodores 1978, Fat Larry's Band 1982
16 The Bee Gees 1968, The Christians 1989
17 Lulu 1964, Tears For Fears 1984
18 Petula Clark 1961, Mr Big 1977
19 Len Barry 1965, Gloria Estefan 1988
20 Little Richard 1957, Kenny Rogers 1977

Answers

 1 *Absolute Beginners*
 2 *After the Love Has Gone*
 3 *I Feel Fine*
 4 *I Wonder*
 5 *Surrender*
 6 *Street Life*
 7 *Stuck On You*
 8 *Only You*
 9 *My Girl*
10 *Temptation*
11 *Venus*
12 *What Is Love?*
13 *Crazy*
14 *Call Me*
15 *Zoom*
16 *Words*
17 *Shout*
18 *Romeo*
19 *1-2-3*
20 *Lucille*

QUICK QUIZ – THEME: CHRISTMAS

All the questions or answers in this quiz contain something associated with the festive season.

Questions

1. Which well known dancer defected to the west in 1961?
2. What is the more common name of the helleborus plant?
3. In which TV show did Robbie Coltrane play a character called Fitz?
4. Who led the Mexican attack on the Alamo in 1836?
5. Who won the best actress Oscar for her part in the film *The Piano*?
6. What is the alternative name of the caribou?
7. Who was Lord Mayor of London three times between 1397 – 1420?
8. Who had a 1991 hit with the song *International Bright Young Thing*?
9. Who was US Secretary of State from 1981-1987?
10. Who played Santa Claus in the classic 1947 Christmas film *Miracle on 34th Street*?
11. What was the real name of film star Mickey Rooney?
12. What is the name of Aladdin's mother?
13. Which traditional Christmas carol contains these lyrics: 'Above thy deep and dreamless sleep the silent stars go by'?
14. What were first distributed by a man called Henry Cole in 1843?
15. Which group had a top ten hit with *Tossing and Turning*?
16. In which film did David Bowie play a prisoner of war?
17. What is the state capital of New Mexico?
18. What was Esther and Abi Ofarim's biggest hit?
19. The story of the Magi or Three Wise Men is found in only one of the four gospels. Which one?
20. Who won a pentathlon gold medal at the Munich Olympic Games?

Answers

1 Rudolf Nureyev
2 Christmas Rose
3 *Cracker*
4 General Santa Anna
5 Holly Hunter
6 Reindeer
7 Dick Whittington
8 Jesus Jones
9 Caspar Weinberger (Caspar was one of the Magi)
10 Edmund Gwenn
11 Joe Yule jnr
12 Widow Twankey
13 *O Little Town Of Bethlehem*
14 Christmas cards
15 The Ivy League
16 *Merry Christmas Mr Lawrence*
17 Santa Fe
18 *Cinderella Rockefella*
19 Matthew
20 Mary Peters

QUICK QUIZ – THEME: SNOOKER

All the answers in this quiz contain a colour used in the game of snooker. As in snooker a red is followed by one of the six colours and the six colours are then taken in sequence, in this quiz the first fourteen questions alternate between red and colour and the last six questions are the colours in sequence from yellow to black.

Questions

1 What is connected to the Mediterranean Sea by the Suez Canal?
2 What is the name given to the hypothetical celestial body which is thought to form after the gravitational collapse of a large star?
3 What name is given to a star of great size and brightness that has a relatively low surface temperature?
4 What is known as 'China's Sorrow'?
5 What was the nickname of the composer Vivaldi?
6 What is the alternative name of lignite?
7 Which Stephen Crane novel was set during the American Civil War?
8 Which award is made to the ship making the fastest Atlantic crossing?
9 By what nickname was Manfred Von Richtofen known?
10 What is the common name given to an aircraft's flight recorder?
11 What is the name of the RAF display team?
12 What name is given to an area of protected open land surrounding a city or town?
13 Which act of 1865 limited the speed of vehicles in towns to 2 mph?
14 By what name were members of the Nazi Party's private army known?
15 Which tropical disease primarily affecting monkeys can be transmitted to man by the bite of a mosquito?

16 On which farm did Anne live in the novels by L M Montgomery?
17 Which American singer is often referred to as 'The godfather of soul'?
18 Which variety of the mineral flourspar is peculiar to the Peak District?
19 Who in a hit song invented medicinal compound?
20 By what name has 19th October 1987 become known in stockmarket circles?

Answers
1 The Red Sea
2 A black hole
3 Red giant
4 The Yellow River
5 The Red Priest
6 Brown coal
7 *The Red Badge of Courage*
8 Blue Riband
9 The Red Baron
10 Black box
11 The Red Arrows
12 Green belt
13 The Red Flag Act
14 Brown Shirts
15 Yellow fever
16 Green Gables
17 James Brown
18 Blue John
19 Lily the Pink
20 Black Monday

QUICK QUIZ – THEME: BIRDS

All the answers in this quiz contain the name of a bird.

Questions
1 Which famous architect designed St Paul's Cathedral?
2 Who won a posthumous Oscar for his part in the film *Network*?
3 What name is given to a score of three under par for a hole in golf?
4 What were the first four words broadcast from the surface of the moon?
5 Which Falkland Islands' airstrip did British troops recapture on 28th May 1982 during the Falklands conflict with Argentina?
6 What was the nickname of singer Edith Piaf?
7 Which American soap starred Jane Wyman and Robert Foxworth?
8 Who wrote about the adventures of Lemuel Gulliver?
9 Which company was founded in 1935 by Allen Lane?
10 Where could you see the ruins of the ancient city of Ephesus?
11 Which 800ft high building in London's Docklands was designed by Cesar Pelli?
12 Which political commentator and presenter was long associated with the television show *Question Time*?
13 Which character did John Wayne play in his Oscar winning film *True Grit*?
14 Who won the world welterweight title from Lloyd Honeygan in 1989?
15 Which song was a number 1 hit for Spitting Image?
16 Which TV comedy show starred Diane Keen and Lewis Collins?
17 Which town in south Bedfordshire stands at the north eastern end of the Vale of Aylesbury?
18 What was the name of Sleepy Hollow's schoolmaster in stories by Washington Irving?
19 Who 'went to sea in a beautiful pea green boat'?

20 Which radio comedy show was set aboard HMS *Troutbridge*?

Answers
1 Sir Christopher Wren
2 Peter Finch
3 Albatross
4 'The Eagle has landed.'
5 Goose Green
6 The Little Sparrow
7 *Falcon Crest*
8 Jonathan Swift
9 Penguin Books
10 Turkey
11 Canary Wharf Tower
12 Sir Robin Day
13 Rooster Cogburn
14 Marlon Starling
15 *The Chicken Song*
16 *The Cuckoo Waltz*
17 Leighton Buzzard
18 Ichabod Crane
19 The owl and the pussycat
20 *The Navy Lark*

QUICK QUIZ – THEME: FLOWERS

All the answers in this quiz contain the name of a flower or shrub.

Questions
1 Which character in the *Dukes of Hazzard* was played by actress Catherine Bach?
2 Which detective was created by Margery Allingham?
3 In which film directed by Woody Allen does an actor step out of a cinema screen and begin a romance with Mia Farrow?
4 Who played Ena Sharples in *Coronation Street*?
5 Which private steam railway operates on a five mile track from Sheffield Park to Horsted Keynes through the countryside of East Sussex?
6 Which song reached number 2 in the charts for the Foundations in 1968?
7 In which 1989 film did Dolly Parton run a beauty salon?
8 Which horse won both the Cheltenham Gold Cup and King George VI Chase in 1989?
9 Which Canadian group had a 1970 top ten hit with the song *Which Way You Goin' Billy*?
10 In Greek mythology, which beautiful youth fell in love with his own reflection?
11 In which thoroughfare did Reginald Perrin live?
12 Which 19th century actress and mistress of the Prince of Wales earned her nickname because she was the daughter of the Dean of Jersey?
13 Who played the incompetent Private Pike in the TV comedy *Dad's Army*?
14 In which 1946 film is Alan Ladd accused of murdering his wife?
15 Who wrote *A Severed Head* (1961) and *The Sea, The Sea* (1978)?
16 What was the name of the man who became British Prime Minister in 1894 as the Earl of Rosebery?

17 What did the King Brothers suggest should be worn with 'a white sport coat'?
18 Which snooker ball is worth six points?
19 Which half of a famous comedy duo was born at Ulverston in the Lake District in 1890?
20 Which is the senior order of chivalry in Scotland?

Answers
 1 Daisy Duke
 2 Albert Campion
 3 *The Purple Rose of Cairo*
 4 Violet Carson
 5 Bluebell Railway
 6 *Build Me Up Buttercup*
 7 *Steel Magnolias*
 8 Desert Orchid
 9 Poppy Family
10 Narcissus
11 Acacia Avenue
12 Lily Langtry (The Jersey Lily)
13 Ian Lavender
14 *The Blue Dahlia*
15 Iris Murdoch
16 Archibald Philip Primrose
17 A pink carnation
18 Pink
19 Stan Laurel
20 Order of the Thistle

QUICK QUIZ – THEME: FIFTY FIFTY

Here there's a fifty fifty chance of getting the right answer, guaranteed!

Questions
1 Which is the name of the two humped camel, Bactrian or Dromedary?
2 Which hangs down, a stalactite or a stalagmite?
3 Which is the red one eyed jack in a pack of playing cards, hearts or diamonds?
4 Which of the Queen's sons has the first names Antony Richard Louis, Prince Edward or Prince Andrew?
5 In which hand does the Statue of Liberty hold a torch, right or left?
6 Which is the longer, the Grand National or the University Boat Race?
7 Which banknote shows a scene from *Romeo and Juliet*, £10 or £20?
8 Is a groundnut another name for a hazel nut or a peanut?
9 What did James Hargreaves invent, spinning mule or spinning jenny?
10 In the story of *Jack and the Beanstalk* what did Jack exchange for the beans from which the beanstalk grew, a cow or a horse?
11 Did David Livingstone discover Lake Victoria or the Victoria Falls?
12 Which is a mounted bullfighter, a picador or a toreador?
13 Which straits separate Australia and Tasmania, Bass Straits or Cook Straits?
14 Who is First Lord of the Treasury, the monarch or the Prime Minister?
15 Is magnesium sulphate the scientific name for baking soda or Epsom salts?
16 What is the maximum possible score in ten pin bowling, 200 or 300?

17 In which book is the birth of Moses, Genesis or Exodus?
18 Is a wherry edible or inedible?
19 Which river flows through Lake Geneva, the Rhine or Rhone?
20 In which hand does the statue of Justice on the Old Bailey hold a sword, right or left?

Answers

1 Bactrian
2 Stalactite
3 Hearts
4 Prince Edward
5 Right
6 Grand National
7 £20
8 Peanut
9 Spinning jenny
10 Cow
11 Victoria Falls (J H Speke discovered Lake Victoria)
12 Picador
13 Bass Straits
14 Prime Minister
15 Epsom salts
16 300
17 Exodus
18 Inedible (it is a type of boat)
19 Rhone
20 Right

QUICK QUIZ – THEME: ANIMALS

All the answers in this quiz contain the name of an animal.

Questions

1 Which term describes a useless possession which is very costly to its owner?
2 Which island lies in the centre of Niagara Falls?
3 In bookmaking slang which word describes an amount of £500?
4 What is the umpire in American football known as because of his uniform?
5 Who is the personification of England?
6 How is Sirius alternatively known?
7 Which jewel did Inspector Clouseau try to recover?
8 What was the real name of the man who said 'Include me out'?
9 What in the American West began in April 1860 and ended the following year?
10 In which film did Paul Newman play a character called Brick?
11 Which small island lies to the south of the Isle of Man?
12 Which song by Survivor was used as the *Rocky* theme tune?
13 In dice games what is a throw of double 1 known as?
14 What is the nickname of American golfer Jack Nicklaus?
15 Which Marx Brothers' film is concerned with an American college football team?
16 Which animal's name do cricketers use to describe a player who is a very poor batsman?
17 Which type of knot is used to shorten a rope temporarily?
18 Which is the most southerly point on the British mainland?
19 On which of Shakespeare's plays was the musical *Kiss Me Kate* based?

20 What was the title of the second top ten hit for Duran Duran?

Answers
1 White elephant
2 Goat Island
3 Monkey
4 Zebra
5 John Bull
6 The Dog Star
7 The Pink Panther
8 Samuel Goldfish (he used the name Sam Goldwyn)
9 Pony Express
10 *Cat on a Hot Tin Roof*
11 Calf of Man
12 *Eye of the Tiger*
13 Snake eyes
14 The golden bear
15 *Horse Feathers*
16 Rabbit
17 Sheepshank
18 Lizard Point
19 *The Taming of the Shrew*
20 *Hungry Like the Wolf*

RIGHT WAY
PUBLISHING POLICY

HOW WE SELECT TITLES
RIGHT WAY consider carefully every deserving manuscript. Where an author is an authority on his subject but an inexperienced writer, we provide first-class editorial help. The standards we set make sure that every **RIGHT WAY** book is practical, easy to understand, concise, informative and delightful to read. Our specialist artists are skilled at creating simple illustrations which augment the text wherever necessary.

CONSISTENT QUALITY
At every reprint our books are updated where appropriate, giving our authors the opportunity to include new information.

FAST DELIVERY
We sell **RIGHT WAY** books to the best bookshops throughout the world. It may be that your bookseller has run out of stock of a particular title. If so, he can order more from us at any time – we have a fine reputation for "same day" despatch, and we supply any order, however small (even a single copy), to any bookseller who has an account with us. We prefer you to buy from your bookseller, as this reminds him of the strong underlying public demand for **RIGHT WAY** books. Readers who live in remote places, or who are housebound, or whose local bookseller is unco-operative, can order direct from us by post.

FREE
If you would like an up-to-date list of all **RIGHT WAY** titles currently available, send a stamped self-addressed envelope to
ELLIOT RIGHT WAY BOOKS,
LOWER KINGSWOOD, TADWORTH, SURREY,
KT20 6TD,U.K.
or visit our web site at www.right-way.co.uk